IS

'BOKO'

HARAM?

Responses to 35 Common Religious Arguments against Conventional "Western Education"

Da'wah Institute of Nigeria

First published in Nigeria,

June 2017/ Ramadan 1438 A.H.

ISBN: **978 – 978 – 54797 – 0 – 6**

Copyright © Islamic Education Trust, 2017/1438.

All rights reserved.

No part of this work may be reproduced in any form, and in any language, without prior written permission from the publisher.

Published by:

Da'wah Institute of Nigeria (DIN),

Islamic Education Trust Headquarters,

PMB 229, Ilmi Avenue, Intermediate Housing Estate,

Minna, Niger State, Nigeria.

+234-803-600-5535, +234-818-102-2146

E-mail: dawahinstitute@gmail.com

Website: www.dawahinstitute.org

Praises For The Book

"The Da'wah Institute should be congratulated for another excellent and well-researched book on this critical topic. Using convincing arguments with evidences from the Qur'an, Hadith and statements of scholars both past and present, the book clears many of the misconceptions some Muslims have about conventional education. It cogently argues the need for investing in and improving our educational system as a collective societal obligation (*fard kifayah*) irrespective of what the education is called. The message of this book needs to also find its way to the grassroots level of our local scholars."

Muhammad Lawal Maidoki, Engr. Tech.,
President, Da'wah Coordination Council of Nigeria;
and
Vice President, Board of Trustees, Global Zakat Union, Khartoum.

"This is an important work that provides the much needed clarity on issues and subjects that are easily misconstrued by some to suppress the legacy of normative Islam and reconstruct its stance on education. Also, the book shines light on the vile justifications used by those ideologically opposed to any and all aspects of Western education and exposes them as ordinary myths. As can be easily seen in the clear explanations provided in the book, with the higher illumination of authentic scriptural proofs and scholars' conclusions, the claim that Islam fundamentally disallows the possibility of mutually acceptable benefits of Western education or that mind development through knowledge that returns from the West cannot be legitimately done in Islam are nothing more than ordinary myths. The great significance of this book therefore is not only in its contents, but also in the time of its release."

Disu Kamor
Executive Chairman, Muslim Public Affairs Centre, MPAC, Nigeria.

"I have gone through this manuscript and found it to be rich and educative for the Muslim Community. The book is useful especially to those willing to know the true position of Islam on the conventional education as it operates in Nigeria. I therefore wish to recommend and endorse the use of the book. Jazakumullahu Khayran"

Bashir Ahmad Yankuzo,
Chief Imam, Federal University of Technology, Minna.

"I sincerely appreciate this giant stride by the Institute. Indeed, the book contains very convincing arguments for whomsoever Allah (SWT) wishes guidance."

Dr. Shehu Abdur-Rahman Aboki,
Senior Lecturer, Department of Islamic Studies, Usman Danfodio University, Sokoto.

"It is evident in our world today that modern education which is referred to as western education or *"Boko"* is a necessity. Any argument that will discourage Muslims or prohibit them from participating in it will certainly lead the Ummah to more evil than good. This study carried out by "DIN" is a welcome development. I wish to recommend the book for use and circulation within and outside our country, Nigeria."

Umar Farooq Abdullahi,
Imam of Bosso Estate Juma'at Mosque; and Director General, Niger State Bureau of Religious Affairs.

"The research is in-depth and apt!"

Aisha Gambo (Esq.)

"Praise to Allah the Exalted for granting the ability of accomplishing this noble project of immense benefit for the Ummah and the entire humanity, over the hues and cry on conventional education. This book would not have come at a better time than now due to its essentiality at this point in time.

I pray that our scholars would produce more of these types of indigenous literatures in order to clear the air on most of the contending issues in the society. Amin."

Dr. Khalid Abubakar Aliyu
Secretary General, Jama'atu Nasril Islam (JNI)

"I have gone through the book, and find it highly comprehensive, well researched and thorough. Whether the issues raised and fears expressed were genuine or not, the responses given and solutions proffered were clear and well backed up with evidences. The language is also simple and clear.

All Muslims, especially Muslim organizations and groups have a duty to call for an urgent review of the Nigerian educational policies to recognize some of these fears and address them to accommodate the sensibilities of Muslims. We all have a responsibility to continuously and committedly call for and ensure the needed reforms take place, as the only way to keep away the exploiters and mischief makers whether internal or external from taking undue advantage of our young Muslims."

Moji Hafsa Bello (Mrs.)
Retired Educationist and CEO, Halal Standard Development Trust, (HASDAT)
"What a brilliant effort!"

Imam Morufu Onike Abdul-Azeez
Chief Missioner, Nasrullahi-l-Fathi Society (NASFAT) Worldwide.

"This book is going to occupy an important niche in the understanding and propagation of Islam. JazakAllahu khairan."

HRH Dr. Yahaya Shonga

"It is abundantly clear that escaping from the dark alley of spiritual squalor, economic void and intimidating moral decadence is only possible through the adoption of fructifying scholarship. Education loathes any compartmentalization, thus, it is a misnomer to talk about western or eastern or any form of education. In advancing the frontiers of human dignity, the inestimable role of education cannot be overemphasized. I salute this effort as I consider this work as a timely response to an irrationality that seeks to permanently hold scholarship and us (the Muslims) in bondage."

Asunogie Nurudeen,
Former National President, Muslim Students' Society of Nigeria (MSSN).

"*Boko* Haram became a monster threatening the growth and survival of Islam in Nigeria by twisting vital doctrines of the faith. In the face of the nationwide consternation that greeted the havocs wreaked by this sect, the task of debunking those false teachings and misleading concepts became paramount. It was anybody's assignment and therefore nobody's duty. Such tasks usually lie fallow, with everybody assuming that it was not a personal responsibility. Therefore, the Islamic Education Trust must be commended for taking up this huge challenge on behalf of the Nigerian Ummah.

This book is a rescue literature material and a saving grace. Its benefits go beyond response to the '*Boko Haram*' doctrinal misadventure. It is capable of reducing extreme and *takfiri* propensities among Muslims, douse tension in pluralistic communities like Nigeria and eliminate terror threats in Western countries. I therefore strongly recommend it to Muslims and non-Muslims, young and old, males and females, all over the world."

Prof. Ishaq Lakin Akintola,
*Professor of Islamic Eschatology; and
Director, Muslim Rights Concern (MURIC).*

Table of Contents

Praises For The Book..4

Acknowledgements...15

Introduction..18

Foreword..24

Preface...29

"MAJOR CONCERNS"...35

   A. ARGUMENTS RELATED TO THE CURRICULUM CONTENT..36

      1. The Anti-Boko Fatwahs...................................36
      2. On the Secular or Non-Muslim Origins of Western Education..42
      3. On Giving Less Attention to Religious Education in Schools...54
      4. On the Absence of Religious Instruction in Some Schools..57
      5. On Teaching the Use of Un-Islamic Medication...60

6. On Teaching of Un-Islamic Medical Procedures…………………………………………….63

7. On Learning Medical Procedures that Expose what Only Allah Should Know…………………………66

8. The Prohibition of Learning Medical Procedures that "Compete with Allah"…………….72

9. Teaching the Theory of Evolution is Un-Islamic……………………………………………………….77

10. Studying Laws Other than Islamic Law……82

11. On Teaching and Learning *Riba* or Interest-based Economics and Finance……………………89

12. On Attending Institutions that Teach Subjects that Are Haram……………………………..101

13. On Restricting the Level and Field of a Woman's Education……………………………….115

B. *THE LEARNING ENVIRONMENT OF EDUCATIONAL INSTITUTIONS…………………………..125*

14. On the Morally Corrupting Environment of Campuses………………………………………….125

15. On Co-education being Immoral and Un-Islamic..132
16. Schools and the Islamic Dress Code.......137
17. Wearing the Face-veil (*Niqab*) in School..145
18. On Serving the Nation instead of Serving Only Allah..148
19. The National Anthem and Pledge and a Muslim's *Shahadah*..................................154
20. Standing up in Respect for Other than Allah is Un-Islamic..158
21. Saluting the Flag as similar to Reverence and Worship of an Idol..................................168
22. Conventional Education is Prejudiced against Islamic Education..................................173
23. Western or Conventional Education amounts to Christianization..................................178
24. Christian Dominated Schools as Christianizing Muslims..................................182
25. The Christian Origin and Identity of Academic Titles..................................183
26. On Titles for Christian Clergy used for Muslim Scholars..................................187

27. On Wearing Academic Gowns of Christian Clergy and Origin..................192

"MINOR CONCERNS"..................................201

28. The Un-Islamic Uniform Requirements for Muslim Boys at Maturity......................202

29. On the Educational System as the "Factory" of a Corrupt Nigeria.....................205

30. On Registration with Government as a Sign of Allegiance with *Kufr*..........................212

31. Making Teachers Stand in Class as a Sign of Disrespect...220

32. On Caliph Umar Discouraging Learning in Other than Arabic.................................223

33. Some Mathematical Symbols are similar to the Cross or Crucifix...............................228

34. On Professors of Islamic Studies who Cannot Recite the Qur'an Properly..................231

35. On the Hadith: "We are an Ummah that is illiterate...nor do we calculate"..................235

Conclusion..240

Other Books By The Publisher..................246

Acknowledgements

Sincere praises and gratitude belong to Allah (SWT), who inspired that this work be carried out for the benefit of His creations, and wills that this book sees the light of day. We thank Him for all we have and are, and beseech Him to shower His endless mercy and blessings upon the noble soul of Prophet Muhammad (p), his household, companions and all those who have, and still are following his example.

Worthy of appreciation are the members of the Research and Training Department of the Da'wah Institute of Nigeria - Muhammad Attahiru Baba-Minna, Teslim Adeyemo, Isma'il Abdulkadir, and Haleemah Ahmad; as well as other volunteers who worked assiduously to ensure the completion of this piece - Aminu Bala, Abdullahi Lamido, Muhammad Jameel Muhammad, Ibrahim Bello, and Sakinah Alhabshi. May Allah accept your efforts and add it to your scale of good deeds.

We also are most grateful for the scholarly and insightful reviews, contributions and endorsements by those who have helped in the improvement of this material. They include HRH Dr. Yahaya Shonga, Prof. Ishaq Lakin Akintola, Asunogie Nurudeen, Engr. Muhammad Lawal Maidoki, Bashir Ahmad Yankuzo, Umar Farooq Abdullahi, Disu Kamor, Aboki, Onike Abdul-Azeez, Muhammad Baman, Yahaya Muhammad, Dr. Khalid Abubakar Aliyu, Aisha Yusuf (Mrs.), Moji Hafsa Bello (Mrs.), amongst others. *Jazakumullahu khayran!*

We immensely appreciate the Director of the Da'wah Institute of Nigeria (DIN), Alhaji Ibrahim Ayobami Yahya as well as other members of DIN and Islamic Education Trust (IET) for their support and contribution. May Allah strengthen you and accept your strivings.

We are profoundly grateful to the National President of the IET, Dr. Sheikh Ahmed Lemu, OON, OFR, as well as the Director General of the IET, Hajiya B. Aisha Lemu, MON, FNAE; for their unrelenting vision for the advancement of Islam and Muslims as well as their continued wise counsel and guidance. May Allah spare your lives on goodness and keep your feet firm on His path.

We pray that the reward of whatever good that comes from this effort goes to everyone who contributed to it, mentioned here or not. While several attempts were made at ensuring the correctness of the content of this book, we take full responsibility for whatever mistakes remain therein, and pray that Allah forgives us for the oversight.

To everyone, we say *Jazakumullahu Khayran*.

Wassalam alaykum warahmatullah wabarakatuhu.

Muhammad Nurudeen Lemu,
Director, Research and Training,
Da'wah Institute of Nigeria, Minna.

Introduction

Three main systems of education have been dominant in Nigeria over the years, namely Indigenous education, Islamic education and Western education. Indigenous education, also called traditional education, refers to the type of education offered in the pre-literate era, within the community, by parents, relatives and community members who possessed specialized skills or abilities in various fields of human endeavour. It was a comprehensive educational system that provided training in physical, moral, intellectual, social and vocational development.

With the advent of Islam in Nigeria, the Islamic educational system was established and by the end of the 11th century, Islamic learning had been well established in the North, and the religion and education had spread to some parts of the South. Aside incorporating Arabic syntax and morphology, Arabic lexicography, *Tafsir* (commentary and interpretation of the Qur'an) and *Tajweed* (correct recitation of the Qur'an), the Islamic educational curriculum also covered other areas of study in economics, social sciences, medicine, pure science, arts and so on. It also extended access to women, and Nana Asmau Dan Fodio is regarded as one of the pioneers of women's education in Nigeria.

Western education, also called secular or conventional education was introduced with the arrival of the Wesleyan Christian Missionaries at Badagry in 1842. The main aim of the missionaries was evangelism and the early mission schools were established in church premises. Thus, education was used as a means of converting Nigerians into various denominations of Christianity. The curriculum content of these mission schools were Religion (Christian Religion), Arithmetic, Reading and Writing, (all in English Language). Other subsidiaries included agriculture, nature study, as well as arts and craft. The main text of reference was the Holy Bible and other related commentaries. There was no separation between the church and the school; and the schoolteachers together with their wives were also the church agents.

The introduction of Western education to the North was met with stiff resistance due to the skepticism of the people, who were predominantly Muslims, about the perceived Christianization of Northern Nigeria by the missionaries through their schools. Thus, Western education developed faster in the South than in the North due to geographical, political and religious reasons.

Geographically, Western education came to Nigeria through the coastal areas, thus those nearest to the coast, the Southerners, were the first to benefit from it. The missionaries, who brought the education, therefore settled first within the southern zone before venturing into the North. Politically, there was a well-structured political system in the North, under the authority of the Sultan of Sokoto, which made the people to be united and resist any move to distort their culture. Religiously, and most importantly, the Islamic religion and culture was well grounded in the North; and this they could not afford to compromise, for whatever benefit.

The word 'Boko' in Hausa language is popularly used to refer to the formal public or private educational system in Nigeria, referred to as Western secular education. It is also used to refer to Western education in all its ramifications along with anything associated with it. 'Haram' is a Hausa word borrowed from Arabic language, meaning Islamically unacceptable, forbidden or prohibited. While "Boko Haram" may therefore be interpreted as meaning that the 'Western' secular education is islamically prohibited, it could also be interpreted to mean that evangelism, deceptively camouflaged as Western education, is islamically unacceptable.

The Muslim leaders in the North successfully resisted the intrusion of Western culture and education for a long time until, through military and administrative efforts of the colonial rulers, conventional education was allowed in Northern Nigeria with the condition that their religion would not be interfered with. However, despite the efforts of successive governments in the country as well as the obvious benefits that can be derived from conventional education, there are still pockets of suburbs in Northern Nigeria today where there is no appreciation for conventional education, usually referred to as 'Boko'. The critics of secular education, hinging most, if not all of their objections on the premises of Islam, have put forth various arguments. This has led to educational backwardness of Northern Nigerians, particularly Muslims, in an era where conventional education is indispensable for individual and communal development. It also serves as a potential for extremist behaviour where those that have adopted conventional education are seen as heretics.

This book is the outcome of a survey conducted by the Da'wah Institute of Nigeria (DIN), to identify the most common arguments that are raised against conventional education, and consequently provide responses to them. Parts A and B focus on the major arguments, which are the most common and most important arguments, used to defend 'Boko' being 'haram' – forbidden. The last part of the material covers the minor arguments which are less common but which are nonetheless used to justify the same.

Being the first edition, we assume that there are more arguments that are yet unidentified, and perhaps better responses to the ones already identified. Hence, we implore our esteemed readers to furnish us with more arguments on this theme as well as better responses in order to improve this material.

Foreword

Alhamdulillah, I have been privileged to witness the efforts of successive governments, non-governmental organizations and several other bodies and individuals at ensuring the penetration, acceptance and adoption of conventional education by Nigerian Muslims for their own individual and societal development.

Despite these efforts however, many arguments have been raised in the past and contemporary arguments keep springing up against conventional, secular or "Western" education. These arguments are used to discourage or prohibit the people, largely Muslims, from going to school or adopting Western education. This has sadly continued to date, in spite of the efforts that several Muslims and Islamic organizations have made to make the conventional educational system more accommodating of Islamic sensibilities.

Challenges to Islam and Muslims posed by the conventional educational system have been identified by Muslims; and a lot has been done by Muslim leaders, administrators, academics and educationists to ensure that conventional education is compatible with Islam; that it no longer has the original colonial Christianizing effect; and that it is accommodating of the teachings of Islam and Muslim sensitivities. In pursuit of this ideal, some Muslims have, in addition to reforming the educational system in ways that are more respectful of Islam, also established private Islamic schools and institutions. Likewise, organizations such as National Association of Teachers of Arabic and Islamic Studies (NATAIS), International Institute for Islamic Thought (IIIT), Muslim Students' Society of Nigeria (MSSN), Ansar-ud-deen Society of Nigeria, *Nasrullahi-l-Fatih* Society (NASFAT), National Council of Muslim Youth Organizations (NACOMYO), Islamic Education Trust (IET), Association of Model Islamic Schools (AMIS) and a host of other organizations have continued to work towards better holistic education for Muslims.

Nonetheless, many old and new arguments have unfortunately continued to circulate at the grassroots, which are commonly used to discourage or prohibit lay Muslims from accepting the conventional "Western" education. These arguments are also sometimes used to justify the superiority of the traditional *Almajiri* system of education. This intentional neglect of conventional education has led to undeniable backwardness among Nigerian Muslims regarding access to education and the quality of education that would meet the needs of contemporary Muslims. The cumulative effect of all these has been the sustained existence of so-called faith-based arguments that continue to impede the socio-economic and religious progress of Muslims.

Medically, there is low level of hygiene, high rate of malnutrition, low response rate to health interventions such as immunization, high rate of maternal and neonatal mortality and morbidity as well as higher incidences of common diseases due to ignorance about balanced diet, hygiene and other simple preventive measures. The pervasive illiteracy also increases poverty level due to lower levels of industrialization as well as resistance to new technologies that would have led to spending less time and energy on tasks cum higher efficiency. Socially, many people have lower levels of awareness of national and global events and can hardly compete with counterparts from other regions on many scales. The high level of illiteracy also leads to religious backwardness, as people who fall prey to these arguments usually become blind followers of some self-acclaimed 'Islamic clerics', leading to various premeditated and accidental misinterpretation of some Islamic teachings.

It is in response to this dire situation that this book has been put together in order to dispel such arguments and the various misconceptions that arise from them; as well as to encourage the mass adoption of our 'refined' conventional, "secular" or "Western" education by Nigerian Muslims specifically, and every agent of communal progress in general.

I am fully convinced that most of the problems facing Muslims in Nigeria are in no small measure, tied to the personal greed, selfishness and quest for followership among some politicians and so-called clerics who take advantage of the ignorance of many among the public to push their selfish and shameless agendas, which lack God-consciousness and any sense of accountability. Therefore, the importance of educational pursuit, Islamic and conventional, cannot be over-emphasized.

It is my prayer that this material would be widely read, translated and circulated through the nooks and crannies of the Muslim society; and motivate more of our scholars to actively encourage Muslims to take conventional education more assiduously and to the highest level, not just as a desirable recommendation but as a religious obligation that is a critical success factor in the uplift of Islam and Muslims in Nigeria and beyond.

Dr. Sheikh Ahmed Lemu, OON, OFR
National President,
Islamic Education Trust, Minna.

Preface

Islam has, from its inception, placed a high premium on education and enjoyed a long and rich intellectual tradition. Knowledge (*'ilm*) occupies a significant position within Islam, and Allah is the source of all knowledge and communication skills, and all praise and credit for it goes to Him – *"who taught by the pen, and taught <u>mankind</u> what he knew not"* (Qur'an 96:4-5); He *"created man and taught him speech (to communicate with)"* (Qur'an 55:3-4); and *"To every community we have sent down laws and ways"* (Qur'an 5:48).

Thus, all knowledge is part of the accumulated human heritage from previous civilizations and cultures – Greek, Indian, Roman, Islamic – and no one can take credit or claim ownership of it all; as every invention is built on earlier knowledge received from others and ultimately from Allah.

During the golden age of the Islamic empire (usually defined as a period between the tenth and thirteenth centuries), at a time when Western Europe was intellectually backward and stagnant, it is historically acknowledged that Islamic scholarship flourished with an impressive openness to the rational sciences, art, and even literature. It was during this period that the Islamic world made most of its contributions to the scientific and artistic world. Ironically, Islamic scholars preserved much of the knowledge of the Greeks that had been prohibited by the Christian world. Other outstanding contributions were made in areas of chemistry, botany, physics, mineralogy, mathematics, and astronomy, etc., as many Muslim thinkers regarded scientific truths as tools for accessing religious truth.

The so-called "conventional", "secular" or "Western education" is simply what has been re-packaged by the "West" after adding to what was received from the heritage of humanity throughout history in various parts of the globe, including that of the Islamic world. It is therefore not American, British or European education, but a culmination of knowledge and legacies from ancient times to date, which can in reality be termed "global education".

The value of knowledge (or education) in Islam is not dependent on its geographical or cultural origins but on the basis of its usefulness and whether it contradicts the clear texts of the Qur'an and authentic Sunnah or not. Based on this and the purposes to which the knowledge will be used for, its acquisition could be an obligation (*fard* or *wajib*), recommended (*mustahab*), merely permissible (*mubah*), discouraged (*makruh*) or forbidden (*haram*). Some knowledge which is critical for the survival needs of a just society is essential (*darurah*) and its acquisition is a collective religious obligation (*fard kifayah*) on Muslims.

Disciplines such as Medicine, Agriculture, Commerce, Security, Education, Engineering, Administration, etc. are essential for the public benefit (*maslahah*) and general survival or absolute necessities (i.e. *daruriyyat*) of a good and just society. These are not merely considered as islamically permissible (*halal*), but a societal or collective obligation (*fard kifayah*) that must be studied. To neglect these aspects of life is a harmful evil (*mafsadah*), which Allah will hold the community (or its leaders) accountable for.

Muslim jurists and scholars maintain that what is a pre-requisite for the performance or realization of an obligation (*fard*) itself becomes regarded as an obligation (*fard*). Since the study and practice of fields such as Agriculture and Medicine are f*ard kifayah* (collective societal obligations), then their prerequisite subjects such as chemistry, biology, geography, mathematics, physics, language, etc. become regarded as obligatory (*fard kifayah)* as well. This is because, without these basic subjects, these professions and many others would cease to fulfill their functions in the effective preservation and promotion of the higher objectives of Islam (*Maqasid al-Shari'ah*) – faith, life, security, intellect, enlightenment, social justice, family, wealth, and peaceful coexistence - in contemporary society.

This reasoning is based on one of the major legal maxims in Islamic jurisprudence, which states that: "Whatever is a prerequisite or necessity for the fulfillment of an obligation (*wajib*) is itself regarded as an obligation (*wajib*)." (*Ma la yatim al-wajib illa bihi fahuwa wajib*).

This book therefore highlights thirty-five (35) arguments that have been used to counter the adoption of conventional education. It goes further to debunk these arguments through well-grounded evidences from the Qur'an, Hadith and statements of scholars – past and contemporary – showing that the argument that '*Boko*' (Western education), is 'haram' (forbidden), is not only baseless and unfounded but cannot also be substantiated. It also acknowledges the need for continuous reform of conventional education generally and the learning environment in particular to further accommodate Islam and Muslim sensibilities, such as allowing female Muslims to wear the divinely prescribed hijab as part of their school uniforms. Similarly, it stresses that pursuing conventional education and the consequent professions related to them are essential for societal advancement, as well as the progress of Islam and Muslims; and therefore can no longer be ignored. Lastly, this book concludes that the pursuit of certain fields of endeavour, such as Medicine and Engineering are collective obligations (*fard kifayah*) and the fact that we currently do not have sufficient experts in these disciplines capable of discharging the necessary responsibilities makes their pursuit an individual obligation (*fard ayn*) and a responsibility of every concerned Muslim.

"MAJOR CONCERNS"

This section focuses on the major arguments used to counter the adoption of formal conventional education. The first part considers arguments related to the curriculum content while the second part considers those related to the learning environment.

A. ARGUMENTS RELATED TO THE CURRICULUM CONTENT

1. The Anti-Boko Fatwahs

> Some Muslims quote Shaikh Dr. Bakr Abu Zaid and a *fatwah* of the Permanent *Fatwah* Council of Saudi (*Lajnah al-Da'imah*)[1] as teaching against attending modern conventional education. What is the correct position of this (or these) scholar(s) on modern education?

The two *fatwahs (verdicts)* cited are taken out of their true contexts and their implications are being extended beyond their original purpose. The relevant portions of the long *fatwah* are:

> "...We invite the Muslim Ummah in line with what the council of senior scholars have said; that they should not enroll their children in the missionary schools…. O you Muslims! Contribute

---
[1] See Bakr bin Abdullah Abu Zaid, *Al-Madaris al-'Alamiyyah*, Dar Ibn Hazm, Cairo, 2006, p.60

to building hospitals, orphanage homes and schools for receiving your brothers, children and the needy among you..."[2]

The prohibition in the *fatwah (verdict)* was actually intended to prevent Muslim children from attending schools run by Western Christian missionaries in Saudi Arabia in particular. It was also meant to encourage Muslims to send their children to attend conventional or modern education in schools run by the Saudi government instead. This was to reduce the Westernization and Christianization of Muslim children and other influences of Christian missionaries via the private educational system.[3]

Shaikh Dr. Bakr Abu Zaid also condemned the use of orphanages and hospitals by missionaries of various schools and "classes", as avenues for their subtle and covert missionary activities. He recommended Muslims to build their own schools based on

---

[2] Bakr bin Abdullah Abu Zaid, *Al-Madaris al-Alamiyyah*, Dar Ibn Hazm, Cairo, 2006, p.66
[3] See Bakr bin Abdullah Abu Zaid, *Al-Madaris al-'Alamiyyah*, Dar Ibn Hazm, Cairo, 2006, p.58

conventional education and reform these to suit their own aspirations for their children.

All the children of Sheikh Bakr Abu Zaid had conventional education in Saudi government schools. Sheikh Dr.Bakr Abu Zaid himself has a PhD from the Institute of Advanced Legal Studies (*Ma'had al-Ali li al-Qada'a*) which is a conventional government university in Saudi.

The *Fatwah* of the Permanent *Fatwah* Council of Saudi ("*Lajnah al-Da'imah*") actually permitted conventional modern/Western education and the learning of English language. It was however critical of co-education and NOT of conventional education per se.

A *fatwah* (pl. *fatāwā*) is a specific legal ruling or verdict that is sensitive to context and which is issued by a Mufti, competent jurist (*Mujtahid*) or council of scholars. It is a scholarly opinion or answer to a religious question for a particular time, place or person, and changes with context.[4] It can be a mere

---

[4] Ibn Qayim al-Jawziyyah, *I'lam al-Muwaqi'in 'an Rabbi al-'Alamin*, Dar Ibn Jawzi, Dammam, 1423AH, v.4, p.337.

reminder of a prescription explicitly stated by the Qur'an or Hadith (which may be binding), or a scholar's determination (*ijtihad*) based on a text that is not explicit, or in the case of a specific situation, for which there is no clear scriptural evidence.[5] In this case, the *ijtihad*[6] (independent juristic reasoning and determination) by the scholar is based on the "secondary sources" of Shari'ah – consensus (*ijma'*), analogical deduction (*qiyas*), public interest (*maslahah*), good custom (*'urf*), juristic discretion (*istihsan*), opinion of a Companion (*ra'yi al-Sahabah*),

---

[5] This explanation of *fatwah* has been drawn for the most part from the following sources: Koutoub Moustapha Sano, *Mu'jam Mustalahāt Usūl al-Fiqh, 'Arabī-Inkilīzī* (Concordance of Jurisprudence Fundamentals Terminology), Damascus: Dār al-Fikr, 2000; Qalaji, Muhammad Rawwas, et. al., *Mu'jam Lughah al-Fuqahā'*, English-French-Arabic, Beirut: Dār al-Nafā'is, 1996; and Deeb al-Khudrawi, *A Dictionary of Islamic Terms, Arabic-English,* Damascus-Beirut: Dār al-Yamāmah, 1995.

[6] According to Kamali, "*Ijtihad* is the most important source of Islamic law next to the Qur'an and the *Sunnah*. The main difference between *ijtihad* and the revealed sources of the *Shari'ah* lies in the fact that *ijtihad* is a continuous process of development whereas divine revelation and prophetic legislation discontinued upon the demise of the Prophet. In this sense, *ijtihad* continues to be the main instrument of interpreting the divine message and relating it to the changing conditions of the Muslim community in its aspirations to attain justice, salvation and truth." Muhammad Hashim Kamali, *Principles of Islamic Jurisprudence*, the Islamic Text Society, Cambridge, 2003, p.468.

etc.[7] This become the basis for a *fatwah* due to either silence or ambiguity in the text (*nass*) of the Qur'an or Sunnah. Consequently, there may be many *fatwahs* (based on *ijtihad*) given by various competent scholars, councils or *muftis* or different communities on a particular issue, and none of them is binding to the exclusion of the others as they are mostly context-specific.[8] It is a *fatwah* that is adopted by the State or a judge (*Hakim* or *Qadi*) that becomes legally binding (*hukum*) on the citizens or those concerned.[9] This is not legally binding on citizens of other communities whose leadership have not endorsed the *fatwah* under consideration.[10]

---

[7] Jasser Auda, *Maqasid al-Shariah as Philosophy of Islamic Law*, IIIT, Herndon, 2008, p.77.
[8] Ibn Qayyim al-Jawziyyah, *I'lam al-Muwaqqi'in 'an Rabbi al-'Alamin*, Dar Ibn Jawzi, Dammam, 1423AH, v.6, p.205; Sheikh Ali Gomaa, *Responding from the Tradition*, Fons Vitae, 2011, p. 22; 'Umar Faruq Abd-Allah, *Islam and the Cultural Imperative*, A Nawawi Foundation Paper, 2004, p.4-6.
[9] Sherman A. Jackson, *Islamic Law and the State: The Constitutional Jurisprudence of Shihab al-Din al-Qarafi*, E.J. Brill, Leiden, The Netherlands, 1996, p.145.
[10] Scholars, such as Imam Malik, are reported to not like answering questions related to *mu'amalat* from distant lands, and would often ask the questioner to "ask your own scholars". See similar views by An-Nawawi, Al-Khatib al-Baghdadi, Ibn Qayyim, Al-Albani, Ibn Uthaimeen, and others regarding the

Even if the *fatwahs* cited from the *ijtihad* of Shaikh Dr. Bakr Abu Zaid (and others) actually did conclude that conventional Western education was prohibited (*haram*) for Muslims, it would not be binding on all Muslims in other communities when there are other scholars who have differed on the same issue. This is besides the fact that it is also not the position of the State concerned.

For this reason, and for the fact that the actual *fatwahs* have been taken out of their original context, the use of these *fatwahs* cannot be a valid basis for the prohibition of conventional education in Nigeria or elsewhere.

---

importance of knowledge of the local context and *'Urf* before a mufti delivers any *fatwah,* discussed in Sa'ad bin Abdullah al-Bariq, *Fatawa al-Fadhaiyyat,* Rabita al-Alam al-Islamiy, Jeddah, p.40-43.

2. On the Secular or Non-Muslim Origins of Western Education

What is the position of Islam on studying conventional education in light of its Western, secular or non-Muslim origins? Are Muslims allowed to be educated by non-Muslims?

Allah is the source of all knowledge, writing and communication skills, and all praise and credit for it goes to Him – "who taught by the pen, and taught mankind what he knew not" (Qur'an 96:4-5) i.e. not only Muslims but mankind in general; He "created man and taught him speech (to communicate with)" (Qur'an 55:3-4); "To every community we have sent down laws and ways" (Qur'an 5:48).

Therefore, all knowledge is part of the accumulated human heritage from all previous civilizations and cultures, and no one can take credit or claim ownership of it all. Every invention is built on earlier knowledge received from others and ultimately from Allah. The so-called "Western Education" is simply what has been re-packaged by the West after adding to what was received from all parts of the world.

The value of knowledge in Islam is not dependent on its geographical or cultural origin but on the basis of its usefulness and whether it contradicts the clear texts of the Qur'an and authentic Sunnah or not.

Based on these and the purposes to which knowledge will be put, its acquisition could be an obligation (*fard* or *wajib*), recommended (*mustahab*), merely permissible (*mubah*), discouraged (*makruh*) or forbidden (*haram*). Some knowledge, which is essential for the survival needs of a just society, is essential and its acquisition is a collective religious obligation (*fard kifayah*) on Muslims.

Those fields such as Medicine, Agriculture, Commerce, Security, Education, etc. that are essential for the public benefit (*maslahah*) and general survival or absolute necessities (i.e. *daruriyyat*) of a good and just society, are not just considered permissible (*halal*), but a societal or collective obligation (*fardkifayah*) that must be studied. To neglect these aspects of life is a harmful evil (*mafsadah*), which the community (or its leaders) will be held accountable for by Allah.

Muslim jurists and scholars maintain that what is a pre-requisite for the performance or realization of an obligation (*fard*) itself becomes regarded as an obligation (*fard*). Thus, if the study and practice of Agriculture and Medicine are *fard kifayah* (collective societal obligations), then their prerequisite subjects such as chemistry, biology, geography, mathematics, physics, and others become regarded as *fard kifayah*. This is because, without these basic subjects, professions like Medicine and Agriculture would cease to fulfill their functions effectively in modern society.

The Prophet Muhammad (p)[11] used knowledge that came from non-Muslim sources if it did not contradict the Qur'an, and especially if it was useful. He also instructed his companions to do the same.

- He accepted an idea from Salman Al-Farisi that originated from a Persian (Faris) military

---

[11] "(pbuh)" stands for "peace be upon him" when used for any of God's Prophets.

defense strategy. This was the idea of digging a trench or ditch (*khandaq*) which was used to protect the city of Madinah from the invading army of the Quraish and their allies during the "Battle of the Trench."[12]

- One of the ways the Prophet (p) offered ransom to some of the prisoners of war after the Battle of Badr was for the Pagan Arab prisoners to secure their freedom by teaching Muslim children literacy.[13]

- He instructed a great companion, Zaid bin Thabit to learn the Hebrew language from Jews.[14]

- He also accepted to be guided through the desert from Makkah to Madinah by Abdullah bin Uraiqit who was a pagan Arab but very

---

[12] Safiy al-Rahman al-Mubarakpuri, *Ar-Rahiq Al-Makhtum (Sealed Nectar)*, Dar-us-Salam Publications, Riyadh, 1996, p.140
[13] Safiy al-Rahman al-Mubarakpuri, *Al-Rahiq Al-Makhtum (Sealed Nectar)*, Dar-us-Salam Publications, Riyadh, 1996, p.105
[14] Sahih al-Bukhari. See also Shaikh 'Attiya Saqr, *Fatwahs Dar al-Ifta' al-Misriyya*, no. 328, May 1997.

knowledgeable about the terrain and directions in the desert.¹⁵

- The Prophet (p) asked a Jewish lady to teach one of his wives literacy.¹⁶

- He (p) decided not to prohibit a husband from having sexual relations with a wife that was breastfeeding a child because he said he had learnt that the Persians and Greeks did it and did not cause them any harm.¹⁷

- The Prophet (p) and his Companions accepted medical guidance and prescriptions from non-Muslim physicians.¹⁸

- He accepted that others knew better than he did in some worldly matters (*"umuru dunyakum"*) related to pre-Islamic agricultural

---

¹⁵*Sahih al-Bukhari*, vol.3, hadith no.464, in *Alim 6.0*
¹⁶Muhammad bin Ali al-Shawkani, *Nayl al-Awtar*, Idarah al-Taba'a al-Muniriya, Damascus, vol.9, p.85
¹⁷ Sahih Muslim, cited in Ibn al-Qayyim al-Jawziyyah, *Miftah Dar al-Sa'adah*, p. 620; also see *Zad al-Mi'ad*, vol. 4 p. 26
¹⁸ Sunan Abu Dawud, 3877

practices such as artificially enhanced cross-pollination.[19]

- In fact, any pre-Islamic (*jahiliyyah*) cultural practices or norms that were beneficial and which did not contradict revelation (*wahy*) were adopted by the Prophet (p) as good custom (*'urf* or *'adah*) and became part of his own practice (*sunnah*). Many Islamic financial instruments for example, such as *musharakah* ("joint" partnership), *mudarabah* ("silent" partnership), *murabahah* (deferred payments), *ijarah* (lease), etc. were pre-Islamic but accepted by Islamic law as part of the *Sunnah*. Consequently, in Islamic jurisprudence, good custom (*'urf*) is in fact regarded as one of the "secondary sources" or

---

[19] In *Sahih Muslim, Sunan Ibn Majah, Sahih Ibn Hibban, Musnad Ahmad* and other sources, the Prophet (pbuh) is reported to have said: "I am only a human: if I command you to do something in your religion, then take it; but if I tell you to do something based on personal opinion, then [realize] that I am only human," and in another narration, "Yet if I inform you of something from Allah, then do it, for indeed I will never convey an untruth on behalf of Allah Mighty and Majestic," and in yet another narration, "You know better of your worldly affairs."

proofs (*adillah*) of law in all the major schools of Islamic jurisprudence (*madhahib*).[20]

The importance of all useful wisdom and knowledge irrespective of where it originates from is emphasized in the Qur'an and Hadith narrations:

- "Wisdom is like the lost property (or animal) of a Believer. He takes it from wherever he finds it";[21]

- Allah created humans into male and female, and into nations and tribes "*li ta'arafu*" so that "*you may know one another*" (Qur'an 49:13);

- Muslims are commanded to "*ask those who know (non-Muslims) if they do not know*" (Qur'an 16:43);

- They are asked to "*travel the earth to learn*" the history of earlier civilizations (Qur'an

---

[20] Al-Shatibi, *Al-Muwafaqat*, 2:213; Abu Zahra, *Malik*, 374-375 – cited in Umar F. Abd-Allah Waymann-Langraf, *Malik and Medina: Islamic Legal Reasoning in the Formative Period*, Brill, Leiden, The Netherlands, 2013, p.137-138.
[21] *Sunan Al-Tirmidhi*, no. 2687; *Ibn Majah*, hadith no. 4169

3:137; 6:11) and to also see how Allah brought His creation into existence (Qur'an 29:20)

- Allah praises those who listen critically and pick what is best from what they learn: *"those who listen to what is said, and go by the best in it."* (Qur'an 39:18)

- The Prophet (p) taught that "Whoever treads on a path in search of knowledge, Allah makes easy for such a person the path to Paradise."[22]

- He (p) also described the difference between a knowledgeable person and an ignorant worshipper as similar to the difference between (the brightness of) a full moon and the stars.[23]

- He (p) taught that, *"God, His angels and all those in Heavens and on Earth, even ants in their hills and fish in the water, call down*

---

[22] Cited in *Riyadh As-Salihin*, 245
[23] *Sunan Abu-Dawud*, Hadith 1631

blessings on those who instruct others in beneficial knowledge".²⁴

- The Prophet Muhammad (p) said, "The search for knowledge is an obligation (*faridah*) upon every Muslim".²⁵

- In many supplications, the Prophet (p) taught Muslims to pray for useful knowledge (*'ilman nafi'an*).²⁶

- The Qur'an and Sunnah did not restrict our sources of worldly (*dunya*) knowledge and Muslims are instructed in broad and general terms to study and observe various natural phenomenon and all of Allah's creation in space, the environment, other creatures and in themselves:

- "And we shall show them our signs over the horizons and within themselves…" (Qur'an 41:53)

---

²⁴*Al-Tirmidhi,* Hadith 422
²⁵*Al-Tirmidhi,* Hadith 74
²⁶*Sahih Muslim.* See also Qur'an 20:114

The Qur'an, the Sunnah and practice of the Prophet's Companions, therefore confirms learning from all these sources!

Imam al-Amin Al-Shinqiti gave four scenarios for Muslims relations with the secular or Western educational system: 1) Accept it completely and uncritically (which he says would be wrong); 2) Reject it completely in spite of its beneficial knowledge (which he also says would be wrong); 3) Accept what is wrong and reject what is beneficial (which he says would obviously be wrong); or 4) Accept critically, taking what is good and useful and discarding what is unacceptable from an Islamic perspective (which he recommends).[27]

There are some teachings found in many school curricular that Muslim scholars and educationists have identified as wrong and which must be corrected as they contradict the ethical teachings of Islam. Even if students are to be exposed to some of these, it is essential that the Islamic perspectives on each be

---

[27] Muhammad al-Amin al-Shinqity, *Adwaul Bayan*, Dar al-Fikr, Labenon, 1995, vol.3, p.505

made known and appreciated. Some of these Islamically reprehensible (*makruh*) or unacceptable (*haram*) teachings found in various subjects include: the disregard for Allah as the ultimate Source and Cause of Creation in especially the **Natural Sciences**; some aspects and interpretation of the theory of evolution in **Biology**; disregard for the superiority of explicit Divine injunction over human judgments in **Law**, **Ethics**, **Public Administration** and **Government**; the promotion of interest or usury (*riba*) as an instrument of financial dealings and profiteering from debt creation; gambling and speculation in financial markets; hoarding and creation of artificial scarcity as ways of maximizing profit in **Business Studies** and **Economics**; various forms of cruelty to livestock in **Agriculture**; environmental pollution and destruction to the detriment of people, other species, and subsequent generations (inter-generational injustice) as offered in various branches of **Engineering**; dismissal of all forms of alternative medicine, some natural remedies, as well as psycho-spiritual healing in **Medicine**, **Pharmacy**, and **Psychology**; socio-economic discrimination and apartheid-like systems of **Urban** and **Regional Studies** and **Management**; sexual lewdness and immorality as means of advertising and entertainment in **Arts**, **Media Studies** and **Marketing**; numerous manipulative and unethical practices, and the superiority of interests over values and ethical principles in **Political Science**; extra-marital and homosexual relations as acceptable alternative family systems in **Social Studies** and **Law**; the disrespect of most indigenous institutions, knowledge and wisdom in preference of foreign and especially Western alternatives; etc.

These are all products of the secular ideology that come with some aspects of the modern Western education. While significant progress has been made in some institutions to correct some or all of these, a lot more still needs to be done by competent Muslims.

The only field of knowledge that most scholars insist must be taught to Muslims by Muslims only, is that related to "religion" or creed and worship, and those fundamental tenets of the faith that only a believer is expected to understand and appreciate with conviction.

3. On Giving Less Attention to Religious Education in Schools

Modern conventional education gives more time and focus to the study of mundane secular subjects than it gives to Islamic Studies. Meanwhile, Allah says in the Qur'an (87: 16-17): *"Nay (behold), ye prefer the life of this world. But the Hereafter is better and more enduring."* Is it therefore not prohibited (and even "disbelief" – *kufr*) to regard such worldly subject as more important than religious studies?

A Muslim should give each responsibility its due attention and not neglect especially those responsibilities that are personal (*fard ayn*). In addition, time should be used wisely on important and worthwhile priorities. While Muslims are encouraged to study as much as they can about their faith, not all knowledge of the *din* of Islam is *fard ayn* which everyone must study. Specialists are needed in other fields as well. There is a minimum amount of knowledge that is *fard ayn*. Once you have this, you are free to do other useful/not harmful things

Because the quantity and volumes of hadith literature are more than the quantity and volumes of the Qur'an does not make it more valuable or more important. Because it takes a student longer to study all the hadith than it does to study the whole Qur'an does not mean it is less important to the student. The time it takes to finish a whole book of *fiqh* is more than it takes to finish reading the Qur'an. However, this does not mean that the extra time spent studying *fiqh* is proof that it is more important.

As Islam is a complete way of life, the study of other subjects that are *mu'amalat* and *fard kifayah* are also part of the *din* of Islam if done for the sake of Allah. These include business, farming, healthcare, security work, etc. The time spent studying these subjects is also time spent learning other important parts of the *din* of Islam. Studying more about this world (*dunya*) with a view to understanding it and improving it is not contrary to the teachings of the *din*.

Because a person is spending more time on the farm or with cattle, selling goods in the market/shop, at work, etc. than he spends studying Qur'an and hadith does not mean that farming is more important than Qur'an or hadith. Each requires different time. Cooking takes more time than eating, even though eating is more important.

The amount of accumulated knowledge in various fields is more than the contents of the Qur'an which does not increase in size, but it does not mean it is more important. Every year, more knowledge from various fields is added to every other subject.

As long as the knowledge is useful and will be put toward fulfillment of worthwhile goals which are acceptable to Allah, then such a person is not committing a sin.

The Objectives (or *Maqasid*) of Shari'ah include the attainment of *tahsiniyyat* (embellishments and luxuries) even though they may not be priorities to some people and they are not as important as *daruriyyat* (dire necessities) or *hajiyyat* (needs).

4. On the Absence of Religious Instruction in Some Schools

> Some schools do not even teach Islamic Studies at all. Is it permissible for Muslims to attend such schools that appear to have no regard for religious instructions?

This argument does not apply to all schools and so cannot be used as an argument against all schools teaching conventional modern education. Many schools teach Islamic Religious Studies to students.

All useful knowledge (*'ilman nafi'an*) that does not contradict clear Islamic teachings is permissible, including that which is "worldly" ("*umuru dunyakum*" - *adaat* and *mu'amalat*). A school that focuses on teaching driving, a vocational training college, school of carpentry, language, etc. cannot be considered *haram* just because they do not teach Qur'anic memorization or Islamic Studies. Because a school has a specialization and is teaching something useful does not mean it is haram.

Likewise, that a school is only teaching Islamic studies and not teaching other subjects that are compulsory (*fard kifayah*), does not mean it is *haram* or deficient either. A school that does not teach religious studies but teaches other useful and essential knowledge is viewed as only concentrating on other subjects, since no school or teacher can teach everything.

A teaching or lesson by a school or teacher does not become blameworthy or *haram* because of what it is not teaching, if what it is already teaching is good and useful. Each can specialize and leave other topics to the more qualified teacher or institution to handle. Some handle one field of topic that is *fard ayn* or *fard kifayah*, while another handles others.

What is important is for Muslim parents and the leadership to ensure that what is not learnt at school or in one school (or through one teacher) is learnt elsewhere – home, afternoon classes, mosque, weekends, holidays, etc. In some places, a student can go to the school in the morning and *Islamiyyah* in the afternoon.

Parents have a critical role to play in ensuring that their children learn their religion - e.g. Qur'an, *Salah*, morals and ethics - from reliable sources.

> Allah says *"Save yourselves and your families from the Fire!"* (Qur'an 66:6)

5. On Teaching the Use of Un-Islamic Medication

> Some medications contain derivatives of pork and alcohol, which are prohibited for Muslims to consume. Is it permissible for Muslims to learn Medicine or Pharmacy from institutions where the use of these products are taught and regarded as permissible?

Not all fields of Medicine and Pharmacy are involved in the use of medication that contains pork derivatives or alcohol. This argument, even if accepted, cannot therefore be used to prohibit the study of Medicine or Pharmacy entirely, which are important for dealing with other ailments and diseases that can be cured without such medication.

A state of dire necessity (or *darurah*) permits a Muslim to consume pork, alcohol, carrion, blood, etc. if there are no alternatives and if that is the only thing that will save a life or give relief. The same verse that has listed some of the various prohibited food, also makes an exception for those facing *darurah*.

> "He has forbidden you only dead animals, and blood, and the flesh of swine... *But if one is compelled by necessity (darurah), neither craving (it) nor transgressing, there is no sin on him indeed, Allah is forgiving, merciful.*"(Qur'an 2:173)

As most people who would need medication that contains pork or alcohol are facing a *darurah* situation, it is therefore permissible for them to use these products if there are no alternatives.

Research for, and knowledge of *halal* alternatives requires experts among Muslims in all the healthcare related fields. It is therefore very important to learn medicine, pharmacy, etc.

There are many other illnesses that need medical doctors and pharmacists. If people do not study these health-related subjects because a very few medications contain alcohol or porcine products, the consequences of no doctors or pharmacists will result in more people dying due to all the other diseases, ailments, accidents, child-birth, etc.

The Qur'an (16:43) advises Muslims to *"Ask those who know if you do not know."* According to Muslim experts and scholars in this field, it is permissible to prescribe such medication containing pork or alcohol if it is definitely necessary and if there are no alternative medicines.[28]

These explanations as well as the statements of many other scholars show that such reasons are not sufficient to prevent Muslims from learning Medicine.[29]

---

[28] This was adopted by the 9th *Fiqh*-Medical Seminar (June 1997) of the International Organisation for Medical Sciences (IOMS), which held that "additive compounds extracted from prohibited animals, or defiled substances that have undergone *istihalah* are clean and permissible for consumption or medicine." - http: www.islamset.org/bioethics/9th*fiqh*.html#1. According to Ibn Hazm, on the subject of *Istihala* (substance transformation), *"The changing of the ruling is by the changing of the name, while the changing of the name is by the changing of it features or properties"* (Ibn Hazm, *Al-Muhalla*, Vol.1, p. 167.)

[29] *Fatwa* of *Mujamma' al-Fiqh al Islami* on learning medicine, cited in Dr. Muhammad Husain al-Jizani, *Fiqh al-Nawazil*, Dar ibn al-Jawzi, Riyadh, Saudi Arabia, 2005, vol.4, p.178

6. On Teaching of Un-Islamic Medical Procedures

> Consumption or ingestion of blood or human flesh is forbidden in Islam. Blood transfusion and organ transplantation is regarded as permissible in modern medicine. This is similar to their ingestion or consumption which is prohibited (*haram*). Is it permissible for Muslims to learn Medicine from institutions where these procedures are taught and regarded as permissible?

This argument, even if accepted, does not apply to all fields of Medicine as not all specializations in Medicine involve blood transfusion or organ donation, such as endocrinology, dentistry, immunology, epidemiology, etc. It can therefore not be used as a basis for prohibiting the study of Medicine or Pharmacy as a whole, but of prohibiting certain practices under certain circumstances.

However, even if blood transfusion and organ transplanting are *haram* – a state of dire necessity (*darurah*) permits eating of carrion, blood, pork according to the Qur'an and the understanding of the consensus of scholars: *"...and the flesh of swine; for that surely is impure"* (Q6:145)."*He has forbidden you only dead animals, and blood, and the flesh of swine...But if one is compelled by necessity (darurah), neither craving (it) nor transgressing, there is no sin on him indeed, Allah is forgiving, merciful."* (Q2:173).

Even if it is haram to perform such operations and procedures, it will still be necessary for doctors to study them in order to assist those facing *darurah* situations – since it is not prohibited for them!

There are other benefits of studying medicine/healthcare which have nothing to do with blood transfusion and organ transplanting and which are even highly needed by the society. Hence, it is not a reason for the prohibition of the study and practice of medicine.

There is also a wrong or mistaken analogy (*qiyas*) being made between the verses prohibiting the diet-related eating, drinking or consumption of pork, carrion, alcohol and the health-related medical procedures of blood transfusion or organ transplanting. As these procedures did not exist at the time of the revelation, the verses quoted are actually silent on blood transfusion and organ transplanting and no scholar of the Qur'an (*Mufassir*) has used them to refer to these medical practices. The context of the verses is clearly related to consumption of food and nutrition. Transfusion is not eating. Adding blood through a vein to the blood inside you is not the same as eating blood just because it goes into you. A woman who receives semen (*maniy*) during sexual intercourse with her husband is not described as having eaten or consumed semen, just because it goes into her through another part of her body!

The Qur'an (16:43) advises Muslims to *"Ask those who know if you do not know."* According to Muslim experts and scholars in this field, blood transfusion and organ transplantation is permissible and the saving of life is a greatly rewarded deed in the sight of Allah.[30]

---

[30] *Journal of Islamic Medical Association of North America*, JIMA: Volume 37, 2005 - Page 38

7. On Learning Medical Procedures that Expose what Only Allah Should Know

> The Prophet (p), in an authentic hadith describes Allah as being the only One Who knows "what is in the wombs". Modern ultrasound scanning of babies in the womb reveals information for doctors to also know "what is in the wombs". These procedures and technologies therefore challenge the authority of the Prophet (p) and the unique knowledge of Allah. Is it permissible for Muslims to learn Medicine from institutions where these procedures are taught and regarded as permissible?

Allah says in the Qur'an (31:34), "*Indeed, Allah [alone] has knowledge of the Hour and sends down the rain and knows what is in the wombs. And no soul perceives what it will earn tomorrow, and no soul perceives in what land it will die. Indeed, Allah is Knowing and Acquainted.*"

In a hadith that is narrated from Abdullah Ibn 'Umar, that Allah's Apostle (p) said, "*Keys of the unseen knowledge are five which nobody knows but Allah...*

nobody knows what will happen tomorrow; nobody knows what is in the womb; nobody knows what he will gain tomorrow; nobody knows at what place he will die; and nobody knows when it will rain."[31]

It is a mistake for anyone to conclude that any advancement in science and technology can challenge the authority of the Prophet (p) or the unique knowledge of Allah. The hadith does not imply that since only Allah "knows what is in the womb", that we know *absolutely nothing* about it – such as whether there is actually a baby (fetus) there or not, whether it is human or something else, etc. Some scholars have concluded based on pure speculation that verse (31:34) and the Prophet (p)'s saying meant that *only* Allah knows the sex or gender of what is in the womb. However, this interpretation and conclusion is not based on the Qur'an or the Sunnah, but on an erroneous assumption attributed to the Qur'an and the words of the Prophet (p).

---

[31]*Sahih al-Bukhari, 4778*

Sheikh Muhammad bin al-Uthaimin clarified the seeming contradiction between the relevant texts and science on this issue and made it clear that there was no real contradiction. He said that such challenges in the meaning of texts occur due to limitations in our understanding of the science or of the relevant texts. He explained how as a fetus grows and develops, Allah allows us to get to know more about it. However, that does not mean that we know everything about it. He cited Ibn Kathir's commentary (*tafsir*) on Surah Luqman (31:34) which states, "No one knows what Allah wants to create in the wombs apart from Him; but once He decrees that it should be male or female, doomed or blessed, the angels who are appointed in charge of it know that, and whoever else He wills among His creation."[32]

The fact that Allah has made it possible for us to know that there is a baby in the womb, that it is a human baby, that it has a beating heart, that it has legs and

---

[32] Muhammad bin Salih al-Uthaimin, *Majmoo' Fataawa wa Rasaa'il Fadeelat al-Shaykh Muhammad ibn Saalih al-'Uthaymeen,* Maktabah al-Shamillah, version 3.13, vol. 1, p.68-70.

can kick, that it is a male or a female, that it is up-side-down (or not), etc. implies that these cannot be what the hadith is referring to. Since the hadith has not specified what exactly it is in the womb that "only Allah knows", it therefore implies that the hadith is referring to the "unseen" aspects of the fetus and something else which we do not know and which only Allah knows. This would therefore be things such as what "fate" (*qadr*), gifts or provisions (*rizq*), and other qualities that Allah has bestowed on the fetus which we definitely do not and cannot know, and which only Allah knows.

This hadith therefore cannot be used as a basis for prohibiting the use or study of medical procedures such as ultrasound scanning, X-rays, MRI, ECG, etc. as these do not in any way challenge the authority of the Prophet (p) or the unique knowledge of Allah. It is in fact by the grace of Allah that humans have arrived at these useful medical technologies that have helped in saving the lives of many mothers and children in ways that were not possible in the past.

It is a mistake to claim that humans can challenge the knowledge of Allah based on our limited understanding of a verse of the Qur'an or hadith or of science and reality.

Ghayb refers to knowledge that is beyond our perception. Some forms of *ghayb* are absolute and known only to Allah, and there is nothing we can do to acquire such knowledge. Other forms of *ghayb* are relative. They are known to some people but not others; to some generations but not others, to some specialists and researchers but not others; to those who have died and left this world but not to others left behind and still alive, etc. Some knowledge therefore will also not be known until the Hereafter.

This explains why every generation of scholars come up with new and sometimes different commentaries (*tafasir*) of certain verses of the Qur'an, and commentaries (*sharh*) of certain hadiths, based on their unique and God-given newly found knowledge, understandings and perspectives of the texts. Therefore, the limitations of one generation cannot be a basis for limiting the understanding and interpretations of the "living text" of the Qur'an (or of the *Sunnah*) by subsequent generations.

Allah is He *"who taught by the pen, and taught mankind what he knew not"* (Qur'an 96:4-5); *"And We (Allah) shall show them Our signs over the horizons and within themselves…"* (Qur'an 41:53)

The fact that someone knows something automatically implies that that knowledge was never a part of "absolute *ghayb*", only "relative *ghayb*", and that Allah has willed that such knowledge will eventually be known.

In addition, scholars such as Muhammad bin Uthaimin have given rulings (*fatwahs*) on the permissibility of using beneficial medical technologies such as ultrasound scanning, etc., and that these do not contradict the main hadith on this topic.[33]

---

[33] Muhammad bin Salih al-Uthaimin, *Majmu' al-Fatwahs*, al-Maktaba al-Shamillah, vol.5, p.198

8. The Prohibition of Learning Medical Procedures that "Compete with Allah"

> Medical procedures such as "In Vitro Fertilization" (IVF) or "Test-tube babies" and abortion are taught in Medical schools. These are prohibited in Islam because they compete with Allah in "giving life and death" (Qur'an 2:258). Is it permissible for Muslims to learn Medicine from institutions where these procedures are taught and regarded as permissible?

If these medical procedures are prohibited because they are viewed as competing with Allah in "giving life and death", then the same logic would make it prohibited for a doctor to give medication to anyone; this will make the whole field of medicine, midwifery, nursing and pharmacy to be prohibited. It will make it prohibited for a Muslim to work in the security services or the military because a soldier will be viewed as also "giving life" to the innocent and "taking life" of the enemy. A mother will be viewed as competing with Allah in "giving life" to her child by breastfeeding it. A judge and executioner will be viewed as competing with Allah in "taking life" of the guilty murderer who also "competes with Allah" in "taking the life" of an innocent person. Allah promises that "whoever takes the life of an innocent person…" is like one who took the life of all humanity; and "whoever save the life of an innocent person…" is like one who saves the life of all humanity! (Qur'an 5:32).

Scholars have therefore understood the phrase "giving life and death" when done by Allah as describing Allah's spiritual act of joining the soul with the body (giving it life) or separating the soul from the body (causing its death). Only Allah can move the soul in or out of a body. Whatever humans may try to do, a person will not live if Allah has decided that the soul will not return. And a person will not die unless Allah decided that the soul will leave the body. It simply means that it is Allah that has the ultimate power over the soul-giving or soul-removing cause of life and death of any of His creatures.

This verse in no way prohibits Muslims from finding ways to achieve the promotion and "preservation of life" (*hifz al-nafs*) which is one of the fundamental objectives (*maqasid*) of Shari'ah based on numerous texts of the Qur'an and Sunnah. Allah however holds us responsible for our attempts to injure, kill or destroy the body in order to make it inhabitable for the soul. He also encourages us to do whatever we can to defend, repair and nourish the body with the various tools, resources and knowledge He has given us, in order to make it more habitable for the soul; and this includes various medicines and medical procedures.

Allah makes it clear that human being "cannot create even a fly" (Qur'an 22:73). Also, when a person's appointed time to die comes, it cannot be delayed nor prolonged by any moment of time (Qur'an 16:61). There is never a competition with Allah. If humans are ever able to do something, it is because Allah has willed that they will be able to: "And you cannot will, except that which Allah has willed…" (Qur'an 81:29. Also, 9:51).

The "giving or taking of life" by humans is only a physical act, by Allah's leave, and is in no way a competition with Allah!

In Vitro Fertilization (IVF) is therefore only a medical procedure – among many other medical procedures - that artificially facilitates fertilization of a sperm and egg when the natural methods do not work. It is therefore viewed as a cure – by Allah's leave - to some (but not all) cases of infertility.

Expert scholars in this field have given *fatwahs (verdicts)* in favour of the permissibility under some circumstances, of In Vitro Fertilization (IVF) as well as abortion.

While these procedures can be abused like any other treatment, there are definitely cases where they are permissible and necessary, and there will be the need for expert doctors and surgeons to perform such operations and procedures. Consequently, there will be the need for Muslim medical students (and especially women!) to study these procedures as part of their (*fard kifayah*) studies in Medicine for the benefit of the Ummah and society as a whole.

The Islamic Fiqh Council (*Majma' al-Fiqh al-Islami*), issued a statement that IVF is permissible if it is done by a married couple without the interference of third party.[34]

---

[34] Dr. Muhammad bin Husain al-Jizani, *Fiqhal-Nawazil*, Dar Ibn Jawzi, 2005, vol.4, p.68-74

9. Teaching the Theory of Evolution is Un-Islamic

> What is Islam's position regarding the Darwinian Theory of Evolution of life? This theory teaches that human being originated from ape-like beings and not from Adam and Eve as the Qur'an teaches. Is the fact that this theory is taught in schools not enough a reason to regard the educational system as prohibited? And is it not prohibited for Muslims to attend schools or classes where this is taught?

Not all schools and teachers teach the Theory of Evolution nor do they all teach it as scientific fact. Some schools and teachers may teach it to students while also educating students on the flaws and disagreements many scientists have with the theory. This argument cannot therefore be used to condemn all schools teaching conventional education or even those teaching biology.

Both scientists and religious scholars have differed in their understanding of the various theories of evolution and their implications. Some understand evolution as a method and process of creation used by God for bringing His creation into existence.[35] Others see evolution as possibly applying to some of God's creation (such as minerals, plants and animals) but not to others (such as humans – Adam and Eve).[36] Some understand it as applying only within a species and creating various races, tribes and varieties but not

---

[35] Muhammad Shahrour, *Al-Kitab wal Qur'an: Qira'a Mu'asirah,* Al-Ahaly, Damascus, Syria,1990, p.281–285; Nidhal Guessoum, *Islam's Quantum Question: Reconciling Muslim Tradition and Modern Science*, I. B. Tauris, London, 2011, p.312-314, 323-324; Ziauddin Sardar, *Reading the Qur'an: The Contemporary Relevance of the Sacred Text of Isalm,* Oxford University Press, New York, 2011, p.359-362; Muhammad Asad, *The Message of the Qur'an,* The Book Foundation, Bristol, UK, 2002, p.1024, n.10. For further readings and references on various views held by other past and present Muslims scholars and authors, see Adel A. Ziadat, *Western Science in the Arab World:The impact of Darwinism*, The Macmillan Press Ltd., London, 1986, p.84-122. See also the comprehensive paper by Prof. Abdul Majid at http://www.irfi.org/articles/articles_151_200/muslim_responses_to_evolution.htm (21/12/2016)

[36] Dr. Israr Ahmad Khan, *The Process of Creation: A Qur'anic Perspective* (Translated By Dr. Absar Ahmad), Markazi Anjuman Khuddam-ul-Quran, Lahore, 2013; Ahmed Afzal: "Quran and Human Evolution", in the *Quranic Horizons,* 1:3, 1996, p.50-51. For further readings on various views held by other past and present Muslims scholars and authors, see Nidhal Guessoum, *Islam's Quantum Question: Reconciling Muslim Tradition and Modern Science*, I. B. Tauris, London, 2011, p.271-324; Adel A. Ziadat, *Western Science in the Arab World:The impact of Darwinism*, The Macmillan Press Ltd., London, 1986, p.84-122.

between species. These therefore accept mutation and adaptation, but completely deny all other forms of evolution and believe that everything came into being through "instantaneous creation" and adaptation to environment through God's will.[37] Many have a combination of these various beliefs. (Some Atheists view evolution as proof that there is no God, while religious people who believe in it (or some of it) view evolution as presenting proof of God's existence). The majority of scholars among Muslims, Christians and Jews believe that Adam and Eve were the first human beings.

Even if one believes that the Theory of Evolution is completely wrong and unacceptable, it is through

---

[37] Mohammed Said Ramadan Al-Bouti, *Kubra al-Yaqiniyyat al-Kawniyyah: Wujud al-Khaliq wa Wadhifat al-Makhluq,* Dar al-Fikr, Damascus, Syria, 2004; Harun Yahya, *Evolution Deceit,* Ta-Ha Publishers, London, 1999; Harun Yayha, *Atlas of Creation*, Vol. 2, 13th ed., Global Publishing, Istanbul, Turkey, 2008; Shihab-ud-Din Nadvi, *The Creation of Adam and the Evolutionary Theory,* Furqani Academy, New Delhi, 2001; Wahiduddin Khan, *God Arises: Evidence of God in Nature and in Science,* Goodword, New Delhi, 1999; Seyyed Hossein Nasr, "On the Question of Biological Origins," *Islam & Science* 4.2, Winter, 2006, p.181–197; Nuh Ha Mim Keller, *Evolution Theory and Islam: Letter to Suleman Ali,* M.A.T. Papers, London, 1999; Muzaffar Iqbal, "On the Sanctity of Species," *Islam & Science* 4.2, Winter, 2006, p.89.

learning and understanding it that one can criticize various positions better, correct misconceptions and give better and more authoritative guidance to others.

Allah praises those who listen critically and pick what is best from what they learn and discard the rest: *"those who listen to what is said, and go by the best in it"* (Qur'an 39:18)

However, the Theory of Evolution is only one topic among many other more important topics in biology that are important prerequisites for studying subjects that are "collective obligations" (*fard kifayah*) in Islam such as Medicine, Agriculture, Pharmacy, etc. Education as a whole and the study of biology in this instance is too important to be abandoned simply because of the existence of a topic such as Theory of Evolution (or any other unacceptable topic), which a student can afford to disbelieve, and teachers can criticize it in a balanced way.

Meanwhile, Muslim scholars should ensure that correct and informed Islamic perspectives on the Theory of Evolution are made available to teachers and students, and that any attempt to discredit the existence of Allah is effectively countered.

10. Studying Laws Other than Islamic Law

Is it permissible for a Muslim to study Common Law or any law other than Islamic Law?

When Muslims live in any place that is governed by laws that are not guided by Islamic teachings, as they did in Abyssinia (Ethiopia) or in Makkah (after the treaty of Hudaibiyyah) during the time of the Prophet (p), they are to work within the existing legal system and peace treaty agreements (*sulh*) to bring about better changes. (Even the King (Negus) of Ethiopia at that time who had embraced Islam was not in a position to implement any other laws other than the customary law of the land.) The Prophet (p) instructed Muslims and their leaders to always honour and stand by the agreements they make: *"Al Muslimun inda shurutihim!"* (Muslims are bound by the conditions they accept), and all believers are characterized in the Qur'an as those *"who are faithful to their trusts and to their pledges"*. (Qur'an 23:8)

During the "Makkan Period" and within the legal and administrative system of the "*Jahiliyyah* society" of

Makkah the Prophet (p) joined a group known as the **Hilf al-Fudul**. This was a group of upright individuals in Makkah who would stand to protect the rights of any victim of oppression in Makkah. Even after Islam was well established, the Prophet (p) recounted his involvement with the Hilf al-Fudul, and according to Talha ibn Abdullah, he said that "if he was to be invited again to join such a group now in the time of Islam, he would respond and join them".[38] According to Ibn Hisham, "They (members of Hilf al-Fudul) promised and pledged that they would not find any oppressed person among their people or among anyone else who entered Makkah except that they would support him. They would stand against whoever oppressed him until the rights of the oppressed were returned."[39] The Prophet (p) was reported by Ibn Abbas as having said, "Every pact (or treaty) from the Time of Ignorance (*Jahiliyyah*) is not

---

[38] Sunan Al-Kubra, no.12114; *Al-Dala'il fi Gharib al-Hadith*, 243
[39] Ibn Hisham, *Sirat an-Nabawiyyah*, 1/123; *Al-Dala'il fi Gharib al-Hadith*, 243

increased by Islam except in strength and affirmation."⁴⁰

Scholars have concluded from this that Muslims, even where they do not control the government or laws of the land, are expected to enjoin right and forbid wrong (as instructed by the Qur'an 3:104) to the best of their abilities (Qur'an 64:16) within the existing societal restrictions. Allah says Muslims should *"Cooperate in righteousness and piety, and do not cooperate in sin and aggression"* (Qur'an 5:2)

Muslims must always have, as a social obligation (*fard kifayah*), those amongst them who will defend the legal rights of other Muslims and victims of abuses and injustice in societies where Islamic law has no jurisdiction. This has most effectively been done through the legal system giving rights to minorities and indigenous people, in the movement to abolish slavery, the Civil Rights Movement for African Americans in the United States, and for the Native Africans in South Africa under the Apartheid Regime,

---

⁴⁰*Musnad Ahmad*, 2904

and many other countries seeking independence from various colonialists.

While this approach can and has been frustratingly slow for many, it appears to have been the most effective, sustainable and successful.

It is therefore important to have Muslim Lawyers and Judge sat the highest level to fight the oppression and abuses against the Muslim community and others where Islamic law does not exist. Muslim participation in all the sectors of the economy and governance generally is a protection against tyranny and domination of Islam and its people. Failure to do so has always resulted in sidelining and oppression of Muslims in all aspects of life, governance and justice. The study and practice of laws other than Islamic laws in these societies is therefore at least a "lesser evil" in the greater public interest of Muslims (*Maslahah*).

A Muslim should never turn away from an opportunity to do good or correct a wrong in any context wherever possible. According to the great jurist Al-Izz bin Abd al-Salam, "When you study how the purpose of law brings good and prevents mischief, you realize that it is unlawful to overlook any common good or support any act of mischief in any situation, even if you have no specific evidence from the script, consensus, or analogy."[41] This is at the heart of Islamic revival, renewal and reform (*Islah* and *tajdid*).

All legal reforms in any society are made by law experts of the highest qualifications. This in turn require Muslims to take the study of law to the highest level. (The same applies to the study of finance and the popularization and legalization of Islamic Finance, etc.)

Even if some laws are wrong and unjust, they need to be studied in order to be identified, understood, challenged and changed by competent legal experts[42]. Muslims are required to study not only knowledge of what is *halal* in order to follow it, but also knowledge of *haram* in order to prevent, avoid or change it. In a

---

[41] Al-Izz bin Abd al-Salam, *Qawa'id al-Ahkam fi Masalih al-Anam*, vol.2, p.160; Cited in Jasser Auda, *Maqasid al-Shari'ah: A Beginner's Guide*, IIIT, London, 2008, p.19

[42] Al-Shaikh Ibn Baaz, *Majmoo' Fataawa*, Maktabah al-Shamilah, vol.2, p.326

well-known supplication (*du'a*), Muslims are taught to pray to Allah to *"Show us the truth (and help us identify it) as truth, and give us the ability to follow it; and show us falsehood (and help us identify it) as falsehood, and give us the ability to keep away from it"*.[43] It is also reported that the Companion of the Prophet (p), Hudhaifah bin Al-Yaman said that, *"people used to ask the Prophet (p) regarding what was good (al-khair), and I used to ask regarding evil (sharr) so as not to be a victim..."*[44]

Not all aspects of Common Law or Customary Law are contrary to Islamic Law. There are many existing laws that do not contradict Islamic law and are acceptable under *'urf* (good custom), *istishab* (the presumption of continuity), *maslahah* (public interest), *ta'zir* (discretionary punishments by a judge), and *ijtihad* (juristic reasoning), etc. There is therefore the need to be specific regarding what particular laws actually contradict Islamic Law, and how to bring about the necessary changes.

---

[43] *Tafsir Ibn Kathir*, vol.1/310; *Tafsir Ruh al-Bayan* vol.8/386; *Al-Wasit li Sayyid Tantawy* vol.1/366, 1623)
[44] *Sahih Bukhari* and *Sahih Muslim*

Sheikh Justice Ahmad Muhammad Shakir is often quoted as being critical of Common Law (in Egypt) where he pushed for many reforms. It should however be remembered that to do so effectively, he had to study law and even become a respected judge in the Egyptian legal system where he worked until his retirement.

11. On Teaching and Learning *Riba* or Interest-based Economics and Finance

> The Qur'an and Sunnah clearly prohibit Muslims from any dealings that involve interest/usury (*riba*). Dealing in usury and interest (*riba*) are part of disbelief (*Kufr*). In conventional education, some subjects and fields require the study of interest or usury (*riba*) which Islam prohibits. Is it permissible for a Muslim to study subjects such as Economics, Accounting and Commerce, etc. that are in preparation for work in conventional banks and financial institutions that deal in *riba*?

There is no doubt that the Qur'an and Sunnah have clearly prohibited dealing in *riba* or interest/usury (Qur'an 2:275). While some scholars continue to differ in their definition and identification of *riba*, the view of the majority is that the interest which modern financial institutions deal with is *riba*, and is therefore prohibited (*haram*).[45]

---

[45] Mohammed Taqi Usmani, *The Text of the Historic Judgement on Riba by Supreme Court Pakistan,* Islamic Book Trust, 2003.

There are an increasing number of Islamic financial institutions in Nigeria such as *Ja'iz* Bank Plc., Lotus Capital (Halal Investments) Ltd., etc. In addition, many conventional banks and financial institutions have opened interest-free "windows" or departments that offer Islamic financial services. Those Muslims who established and manage these institutions acquired their expertise, experience, skills and knowledge of finance and the market from studying how the *riba*-based economy and companies work, and finding creative ways of establishing Islamically viable alternatives. So even if Muslims would want to study for work in Islamic financial institutions, they will still have to study all the subjects needed for qualifying to work in conventional financial institutions since most of the subject are not purely related to *riba* dealings per se, but to do with running any kind of financial services organization, Islamic or otherwise – be it an equity investment company, insurance, bank, pension fund, or any other business. Most Islamic financial instruments and products are only slight modifications of many of those used in the conventional institutions.

If you don't study and understand a disease and its environment, it becomes difficult to recommend or prescribe an effective cure. How can you fight an enemy that you don't want to know? If concerned Muslims are prohibited from studying conventional *riba*-based finance and economics, and are also forbidden from gaining adequate working experience in the leadership and management of successful conventional *riba*-based companies, where else will the Muslim Ummah get the good and competent men and women who can establish and run viable and sustainable *halal* alternatives that can out-compete the existing *riba*-based systems?

Knowledge of *halal* and *haram* is essential in knowing what to do and acquire, and what to avoid and how to avoid it. The study of how *riba* works and why it has become so widespread is essential for finding viable and competitive Islamic alternatives. This knowledge is also important in identifying how to collaborate with conventional financial institutions in ways that are Islamically acceptable. It is also necessary for understanding how to identify (prohibited) legal stratagems (*hiyal*) and prevent or sanction them.

Nearly all pioneers of Islamic financial institutions have had to study, work and succeed in running successful *riba*-based institutions before they could acquire the credibility in the eyes of even Muslim investors and be trusted to establish Islamic alternatives that would also succeed and be attractively profitable. This is especially so as the economic environment is naturally more hostile to new competitors, and particularly those such as Islamic financial institutions.

In a society where there is no viable or easily accessible alternative to usury (*riba*) sources of capital (or credit loans), many scholars allow a concession (*rukhsah*) for Muslims who have important needs (*haajah*) so that the community as a whole (especially the poor) does not fall into desperation or a state of emergency or dire necessity (*darurah*) when such *riba* would become temporarily permissible.[46] Allah says:

---

[46] See references to the various scholars and Fatwa Councils and the arguments they proffer in Sheikh Yusuf al-Qaradawi, *Fiqh of*

"But if one is compelled by necessity (darurah), neither craving (it) nor transgressing, there is no sin on him indeed, Allah is forgiving, merciful." (Qur'an 2:173).

The Prophet Muhammad (p) taught that *"Whoever sees something that is wrong, should change (or correct) it with his hands,...or his tongue, ...or his heart."*[47] In other words, a Muslim must try to change what is wrong and replace it with a better alternative or lesser evil. It is not sufficient for Muslims to only condemn what is wrong. Instead of abusing and criticizing the darkness, one should be constructive and light a candle!

Economic reforms at all levels are made by experts of the highest qualifications and authority, which requires the study of economics, finance, commerce, banking, insurance, etc., as can be seen from the

---

Muslim Minorities: Contentious Issues and Recommended Solutions, Al-Falah Foundation, Cairo, Egypt, 1424.2003, p.152-199. See other classical and contemporary scholars and their arguments cited in Khaled Abou El Fadl, "Islamic Law and Muslim Minorities: The Juristic Discourse on Muslim Minorities from the Second/Eighth to the Eleventh/Seventeenth Centuries", in *Islamic Law and Society*, E.J. Brill, Leiden, Vol. 1, No. 2, 1994, p.181-187.

[47] *Sahih Muslim*

experience of many countries. A Muslim should study to the highest level and work with the intention of bringing positive reform to any and all sectors of the economy that needs improvement, however small that change may be. This role is a collective religious obligation (*fard kifayah*).

There are many poverty-alleviating programmes and credit opportunities made available for everyone but which Muslims do not benefit from simply because they are not packaged in ways that are halal. This is often because there are insufficient competent Muslims at the top who can ensure that tax-paying Muslim citizens also benefit from government welfare packages. This is especially important as the majority of poor people in Nigeria are among the Muslims. This urgently needed reform makes the study of conventional economics and finance to the highest level a collective religious obligation (*fard kifayah*)! This was actually how the former Governor of the Central Bank of Nigeria, HRH. Sanusi Lamido Sanusi II, was able to make important policy and structural changes at the CBN that facilitated the oversight, governance and greater formal recognition of Islamic Financial Institutions in Nigeria. Consequently, the CBN now has a very competent Shari'ah Advisory Board made up of some of the most respected Islamic scholars in Nigeria.

In an environment where *halal* alternatives are scarce or absent, it is important for Muslim economists to ensure that they are able to protect the Muslim community and individuals against economic exploitation, oppression and abuses of especially the less privileged, and to any degree possible. Muslims' participation at the highest levels and in all the sectors of the economy and its governance is a way of protecting Muslims from tyranny and economic subjugation by islamophobes and enemies of Islam. This role is also a collective religious obligation (*fard kifayah*).

Failure to become leaders or positively influence the leadership in any aspect of life exposes Muslims to discrimination and bigoted policies of others, which in turn creates resentment, frustration and interfaith tension.

Muslim jurists and scholars (of *Usul al-Fiqh*) maintain that what is a pre-requisite for the performance or realization of an obligation (*fard*) itself becomes regarded as an obligation (*fard*). Hence, the pre-requisite education, degrees, certification and working experience required to fulfill a *fard kifayah* are themselves regarded as *fard kifayah*. Without these, the Ummah slides into a state of dire necessity (*darurah*) which then makes the *haram* (*riba*) permissible.

Scholars (for example) agree based on clear text from the Qur'an and Sunnah, that theft (*sariqa*) is categorically prohibited (*haram*). They however differ in its definition and whether *sariqa* is the same as embezzlement, pickpocketing, bribery, money laundering, etc. and therefore carries the same punishment.[48] So, while the Qur'an is clear on the

---

[48] See Ministry of *Awqaf* and Religious Affairs, *Al-Mausu'ah al-Fiqhiyyah al-Kuwaitiyyah*, Dar al-Salasil, Kuwait, 1424AH, vol.24, p.293; vol.24, p.259; vol.24, p.307, for more discussion of the differing views of classical scholars on the definition of *sariqa*. Also, Mohamed S. El-Awa, *Punishment in Islamic Law*, American Trust Publications, U.S., 1993.

prohibition of *sariqa*, scholars differ on the precise definition and the scope of its application.

Similarly, while the prohibition of *riba* is clear and accepted by all scholars, classical and contemporary scholars differ on its precise definition and the scope of its application.[49] The commonly held traditional view is that *riba* is simply interest, i.e. any increase in the loan required by the lender as a condition for

---

[49] Muhammad Ibn Rushd al-Hafid, *Bidayat al-Mujtahid*, vol.1, part 2 (Cairo, n.d.); Dr. Ahmad Shafaat, *Islamic Perspectives: What is Riba?*, 2005, cited in http://www.islamicperspectives.com/RibaIntro.htm (visited 04/08/2016); Farhad Nomani, *The Interpretative Debate of the Classical Islamic Jurists on Riba (Usury)*, The American University of Paris, Source: http://www.luc.edu/orgs/meea/volume4/NomaniRevised.htm (Accessed 04/08/2016), etc. Some of these differences of opinion on the definition and scope of *riba* date back to the time of the Companions. Usamah ibn Zayd narrated that the Prophet (pbuh) said: "There is no *riba* except in *nasi'ah* (waiting)"; in another narration: "There is no *riba* in hand-to-hand (on the spot) transactions". (Al-Nasa'i, 50); Caliph Umar said that there were three issues he wished that the Prophet (pbuh) could have explained to them in more detail. Two of them were about Inheritance Law of Islam and the third one was about *riba*. (See Bukhari, 5588; Muslim, 7744; Abu Dawud, 3671; and al-Baihaqi, 5456. Reported also in *Al-Tafsir Ibn Kathir*). On another occasion, he said that since some kinds of *riba* were not quite clear to them (Muslims at that time), therefore they had left almost 90 percent of otherwise permissible transactions in fear of involving in *riba* even unknowingly. (Reported in *Al-Kanz al-Ummal* by Muttaqa al-Hindi).

advancing the loan. It is usually a pre-determined percentage of the value of the capital amount, as opposed to a percentage of the profit (profit-sharing) which is not *riba* in the view of the majority.

Some scholars do not regard the present bank interest to be the same as the *riba* that is prohibited in the Qur'an or Sunnah. Some of them do not apply the concept of *riba* to anything other than silver and gold. Others apply it only to measurable quantities and not quality or value. Others distinguish between "fair interest" rates and "exploitative usury". They do not regard the modern conventional bank interest to be the same as *riba* if it is not exploitative (*usury*), or if it is not at rates that are much higher than the rate of inflation. The view of the majority is that the interest which modern financial institutions deal with is *riba*, and is therefore prohibited (*haram*).[50] While some scholars take very strong positions of these differences, it cannot be denied that there are differing opinions on the definition and application of *riba*. Such differences in interpretation, like many

---

[50] Mohammed Taqi Usmani, *The Text of the Historic Judgement on Riba by Supreme Court Pakistan,* Islamic Book Trust, 2003.

others upon which scholars differ, demand Muslims to exercise mutual respect and the ethics of disagreement. These differences should not be basis for condemnation and disunity.

While the consumption or dealing in *riba* in the presence of viable alternatives is regarded as a sin by all scholars, it does not become an act of disbelief (*Kufr*), unless the Muslim concerned also rejects the fact that the Qur'an regards *riba* as *haram*. Committing a sin (*ithm*) such as stealing, telling lies, breaking promises, gambling, dealing in *riba*, kidnapping, and bribery, etc. are condemned by the Shari'ah. The person who does these acts is involved in wrong-doing (*fisq*), but he or she is not regarded as a disbeliever (*kafir*) according to the earliest generation of Muslims (*salaf*) and scholars of mainstream Muslims (*Ahl al-Sunnah wa al-jama'ah*). Such a Muslim remains a Muslim though he may be treated as a wrongdoer (*fasiq*).

Distinguished scholars such as Sheikh Abdullah Bin Baz have given rulings in favour of learning of economics even if it contains teaching *Riba*.[51]

Muslims in the "Halal Industry" have been working steadily in the areas of banking and finance, food and beverages, hotels, tourism, entertainment, transport, manufacturing, cosmetics, pharmaceuticals, etc. to ensure greater respect for Islamic guidelines and ethics.[52]

---

[51] Al-Shaikh bin Baaz, *Majmu' Fataawa*, Maktabah al-Shamila, vol.2, p.326
[52] Mohammad Hashim Kamali, *The Parameters of Halal and Haram in Shari'ah and the Halal Industry*, Occasional Papers Series 23, IIAIS and IIIT Malaysia, 2013.

12. On Attending Institutions that Teach Subjects that Are Haram

> Some educational institutions offer courses which teach Fine Art (and drawing of animate creatures), un-Islamic Music, Atheistic or Secular Philosophy, Sex Education (for unmarried), and Common Law (which is un-Islamic). Is it permissible for Muslims to enroll in such courses or attend such institutions?

The response to this question is in many ways similar to Question No. 10: Studying Laws other than Islamic Law.

Not all educational institutions teach course contents that are wrong or un-Islamic, nor use methods that are prohibited (*haram*). Even if learning these are regarded as prohibited, it does not prevent a person from learning other courses and subjects that are permissible. Also, a problem with one subject or course or topic does not negate the relevance and importance of other subjects, courses and topics. This therefore cannot be used as an argument to make the whole of conventional education prohibited.

As discussed earlier, it is important in Islam to learn knowledge of both *halal* and *haram*–which will be useful. Even if some subjects or topic being taught are wrong, indecent or unjust, they still usually need to be studied in order to be identified, understood, challenged and changed by competent experts. Muslims are required to study not only knowledge of what is *halal* in order to follow it, but also knowledge of *haram* in order to prevent, avoid or change it. In a well-known supplication (*du'a*), Muslims are taught to pray for Allah to *"Show us the truth (and help us identify it) as truth, and give us the ability to follow it; and show us falsehood (and help us identify it) as falsehood, and give us the ability to keep away from it"*.[53] It is also reported that the Companion of the Prophet (p), Hudhaifa bin Al-Yaman said that *"people used to ask the Prophet (p) regarding what was good (al-khair), and I used to ask regarding evil (sharr) so as not to be a victim..."*[54] Learning something that is false or unethical is not in itself prohibited if it is being

---

[53]*Tafsir Ibn Kathir*, vol.1/310; *Tafsir Ruh al-Bayan* vol.8/386; *Al-Wasit li Sayyid Tantawy* vol.1/366, 1623
[54]*Sahih Bukhari* and *Sahih Muslim*

learnt for the purpose of preventing the wrong or decreasing its effect. What is wrong is the use to which any knowledge is put and not the knowledge itself.

Only sufficiently educated and recognized authorities can effectively and sustainably modify a system to be better, or at least a "lesser evil". In other words, you still need education to change a wrong system.

Weighing between the benefit and harm of education, it becomes evident that it is wrong to discard the greater benefit of education because of a few lesser evil/harm (associated with some topics in some courses). Some examples are:

- The Prophet's (p) respectful treatment of the hypocrites of Madinah (*munafiqun*) in spite of their treachery,

- Not rebelling against even unjust leaders[55] for fear of more damaging consequences to the common good.[56]

- Factors to consider in assessment of harms and benefits - scope and people affected, intensity of suffering caused, probability of long-term intergenerational impact

- **Regarding learning those aspects of Common Law** that are Islamically unacceptable for Muslims

    - It is not forbidden (*haram*) to learn about what is *haram*. It is only *haram* to use the knowledge when there are better, available and applicable *halal* alternatives.

    - Only authorities in law can modify the legal system to a lesser evil and protect Muslims and others.[57]

---

[55]Musnad Ahmad, no. 8953; Sahih Muslim, no. 4860.; Al-Baihaqi, *Sunan al-Kubrah*, no. 16401; al-Tabarani, *Al-mu'jam al-Kabir*, no. vol.22, p.16; *Sahih Muslim*, no. 4888; *Sunan al-Kubrah*, no. 16401.

[56]Ibn Abi al-'Izz, *Commentary on the Creed of Tahawi*, Imam Muhammad bin Saud Islamic University, Riyadh, KSA, 2000, p.330

- **Regarding learning Secular Philosophy**

  - It is not *haram* to learn about what is *haram*. It is only *haram* to use the knowledge when there are better, available and applicable *halal* alternatives.

  - Knowledge of *haram* is *halal* to learn in order to understand and debunk it and protect Muslims and others from its harm, as was done in the past by scholars such as Imam al-Ghazzali, Ibn Rushd, Ibn Taimiyyah, etc.

  - It is important to have experts in *Kalam* (Islamic theology and philosophy) for defense of the religion from corrupt and misguided ideologies. This is actually a collective social obligation (*fard kifayah*).

- **Regarding the learning of Sex Education**

  - It is not *haram* to learn about what is *haram*, in order to avoid it or to protect others. It is

---

[57] See more discussion on this in Question No.10: Studying Laws other than Islamic Law, discussed above.

only *haram* to use the knowledge when there are better, available and applicable *halal* alternatives.

- Islam is a complete way of life and Muslims must be properly guided and educated about sex and sexuality in order to protect themselves from harm, know how best to enjoy legitimate/*halal* sexual relations within marriage, and give guidance to others – especially young people who are surrounded by modern sexual temptations and misguidance.

- It has been shown that sex education is important before and after marriage.

- Sex education is not intended to be about teaching immorality but about giving useful guidance on sexual matters. There is the need to be specific about what is Islamically unacceptable and what is not, and to correct constructively and effectively with knowledge and authority.

- All knowledge is open to abuse, and some will and do misuse it. This cannot be prevented, but can be minimized through holistic approaches by the different stakeholders.

- There is the need for Muslims to also be proactive in guiding the curriculum context and teaching methods of Sex Education in schools.[58] Concerned Muslim parents and relevant organizations should also be involved and give constructive guidance to topics related to appropriate and inappropriate teachings, methods, resources and audience. Not just complaining about the problem, but offering solutions and "changing with your hand...tongue...or heart".[59]

---

[58] A well-researched material specifically for Muslims on this subject matter include – Hisham Al-Talib, Abdulhamid Abu Sulaiman & Omar Al-Talib, *Sex and Sex Education: What Do We Tell Our Children?* The International Institute of Islamic Thought (IIIT), USA, 2014.

[59] Bukhari and Muslim

- The Qur'an and Sunnah have given guidance on sex and sexuality, and a number of respected scholars have written about it.[60]

- With the increase in social and moral problems as well as sexual exploitation, there is a real need to protect young Muslims against misinformation about sex from the media, peers and others. This is especially important when there are those who want to promote ideas about sex and sexuality that are immoral and islamically unacceptable.

- **Regarding the learning of Fine Art**

    - Most of Fine Art is not about drawing or sculpture of complete animate beings, which many scholars regard as prohibited (*haram*).

---

[60] Muhammad Ibn Adam Al-Kawthari, *Islamic Guide to Sexual Relations*, Huma Press, UK, 2008; Ibn Qayyim, *Rawdatul Muhibbeen wa nuzhat al-Mushtaqin*, Dar al-Kutub al-'Ilmiyyah, Beirut, 1992; Abd al-Rahman bin Abubakr al-Suyuti, *Shaqaiq al-Utruj ala Raqaiq al-Ganj,* Dar al-Kitab al-Araby, Damascus; Muhammad Hassan, Muhammad Mukhtar and Muhammad Sa'id, *Funun Fi Ghurfati Nawm*, Maktabat alfa al-Tijariya, Cairo, 1426AH; Salah al-Deen al-Safadi, *Lawatu al-Shaki wa Dam'atu al-Baki,* al-Maktabatu al-Rahmaniyya, Cairo, 1922.

- The fact that the Prophet (p) permitted Aisha to have and play with a toy winged-horse[61] (a sculpture of an animate being) is understood by some respected scholars[62] to imply that the prohibition is therefore only related to the misuse and unacceptable purpose of the sculpture or piece of art of animate beings. Any work of art that will lead to or can be associated with idolatry (*shirk*) is what is clearly prohibited (*haram*).[63]

- Illustrations and art have also proven essential as teaching aids in education, book design, cartoons, children entertainment, notice boards, calligraphy, painting, logos, digital art, learning medicine, anatomy, teaching biology (zoology and botany), geography,

---

[61] Bukhari, 6130; Muslim, 6441; Musnad Ahmad, 24298; Abu Dawud, 4933

[62] Wahbah al-Zuhayli, *al-Fiqh al-Islami wa Adilatuhu*, Dar al-Fikr, Damascus, vol.4, p.223; Abu Muhammad Ali bin Hazm, *al-Muhalla bi al-Athar*, al-Maktabah al-Shamilla 3.13, vol.9, p.26, Issue no.349; Ministry of Awqaf and Religious Affairs, *al-Mawsu'at al-Fiqhiyyah al-Kuwaitiyyah*, Dar al-Salasil, Kuwait, 1404AH, vol.12, p.112

[63] See also Yusuf al-Qaradawi, *Diversion and Arts in Islam*, Islamic Inc. Publishing and Distribution, Egypt, 1998.

- designs of technology, security identification, etc.

- Importance of Visual Arts – No economy can sell products that are not well designed by qualified artists – cars, aero planes, signboards, maps, phones, technology, equipment, books, magazines, CDs, DVDs, posters, adverts, logos, apps, websites, cloth, mats, furniture, etc.

- There should be more *da'wah* for Muslims to be cognizant of *haram* and avoid misusing their qualifications in Art for immoral purposes.

- A whole subject, course or education should not be discarded because of some harmful or non-beneficial parts – if the long-term benefits of such an education are greater than the harm – choice of "lesser evil"!

- **Regarding the learning of Music**

    o There is general permissibility of poetry and songs that are not accompanied by instruments, so long as the lyrics are *halal*, and there is no association with a prohibition. Some of these were part of the *sunnah* and performed during the time of the Prophet (p) and his companions on various occasions.[64]

    o There is also a consensus among scholars that all immoral lyrics and those that encourage wrongdoing are prohibited (*haram*).

    o Respected scholars have differed on the permissibility of certain instruments such as wind and string instruments. While some

---

[64] I.R. Al-Faruqi, and L.L. Al-Faruqi, "*Handasah Al-Sawt* (or The Art of Sound)", in *The Cultural Atlas of Islam*, Macmillan, NY, 1986; Yusuf al-Qaradawi, *Fatawi al-Mu'asirah,* Al-Mansura, Dar al-Wafa', Egypt, Vol.2, 1996; Yusuf al-Qaradawi, *Diversion and Arts in Islam*, (Trans. Rawaa al-Khateab), Islamic Inc. Publishers, n.d.; Isma'il R. al-Faruqi (edt.), "The Shari'ah of Music and Musicians", in *Islamic Thought and Culture: Papers presented to the Islamic Studies Group of the America Academy of Religion*, IIIT, 1982; Sheikh Muhammad al-Ghazali, *As-Sunnan Nabawiyya Bayna Ahl al-Fiqh wa Ahl al-Hadith,* Dar Shuruq, Cairo,1996.

have regarded these as permitted, others have regarded them as prohibited.[65]

- Sufyan At-Thawri[66] was reported to have said, "*If you see a man doing something over which there is difference of opinion among scholars, and which you believe to be forbidden, you should not forbid him from doing it.*"[67]

- Cognizance should be taken of the importance of "*halal* music" (depending on the scholars) in modern media programmes as an aid to

---

[65] See Ibn Taymiyyah "Kitab al-Sama' wal-Raqs," *Majmoo'ah al-Rasa'il al-Kubra,* Matba'ah Muhammad 'Ali Subayh, Cairo, 1966, Vol. 2, p.295-330; Imam Shawkani, *Nayl al-Awtar*, Vol.8, p.264-266; Al-Shafi'i, *Kitab al-Umm*, Bulaq, Cairo, 1906, Vol. 6, p.215; For more discussion of various views on this, seeI.R. Al-Faruqi, and L.L. Al-Faruqi, "Handasah Al-Sawt (or The Art of Sound)", in *The Cultural Atlas of Islam*, Macmillan, NY, 1986; Muhammad Nasirudeen al-Albani, *Tahrim Alat al-Tarab*, Maktabat al-Dalil, 1416, (Maktabat al-Shalimah);Yusuf al-Qaradawi, *Fatawi al-Mu'asira,* Al-Mansura, Dar al-Wafa', Egypt, Vol.2, 1996; Yusuf al-Qaradawi, *Diversion and Arts in Islam*, (Trans. Rawaa al-Khateab), Islamic Inc. Publishers, n.d.

[66] He was also called the "Amir al Mu'minin fi al Hadith" ("Leader of the Believer in Hadith") and was among the greatest scholars of the successors (*tabi'un*) of the companions of the Prophet (pbuh).

[67] Quoted in Abdal Hakim Murad, *Understanding the Four Madhhabs*, Cambridge: Muslim Academic Trust, 1999, p.13).

retaining the attention of viewers and listeners.

- o Halal music and *nashids* need to be taught for various occasions. Even though these are among the *Tahsiniyyat* (embellishments and luxuries) and are therefore not priorities, they still belong among the *maqasid* (objectives) of Shari'ah and are permissible (*halal*).

- o Muslims need to provide alternatives to those forms of music that are clearly prohibited (*haram*), even if some would view this as just a "lesser evil".

- o Allah praises those who listen critically and pick what is best from what they learn: *"those who listen to what is said, and go by the best in it."* (Qur'an 39:18) - Take the *halal* and avoid the *haram*, to the best of your ability.

- o There should be more *da'wah* to Muslims about ensuring the *nashid*s in the music industry focus towards greater God-consciousness. The industry should also be more responsible in their choices of instruments and voices.

- A whole subject, course or education should not be discarded because of some harmful or non-beneficial parts – if the long-term benefits of such an education are greater than the harm – choice of "lesser evil"!

13. On Restricting the Level and Field of a Woman's Education

Is it permissible or necessary for a Muslim woman to learn subjects other than religious studies? And is there a limit to the level of education a devout Muslim woman should attain?

Aisha bint Abu Bakr, the wife of the Prophet Muhammad (p) was among the most respected scholars among the Companions of the Prophet (p) even though she was a woman. Nana Asma'u, the daughter of Sheikh Uthman bin Fodio (of the Sokoto Caliphate) was also one of the most learned people of her time. In Islamic history, there were many scholars whose teachers and colleagues were women. A number of well-respected scholars studied with women - al-Sakhawi (studied with 46 women), Ibn Hajar al-Asqalani (53), al-Suyuti (33). Al-Sakhawi lists 1,075 notable women, 405 of whom were scholars of tradition (Hadith) and jurisprudence (*Fiqh*). Ibn Hajar lists 168 female teachers of tradition and law.[68]

Other distinguished male scholars who also studied from women include Imam Muhammad bin Shihab al-Zuhri who learnt from Amrah bint Abdurahman;[69] Imam Malik bin Anas who learnt Hadith from Fatima bint Sad Al-Madaniyyah;[70] Abul Muzafar al-Samani, Khatib al-Bagadadi and Abu Abdullah Muhammad bin Abi Nasr al-Humaidi al-Zahiri all studied from Karima al-Mirwaziya;[71] Al-Diya al-Maqdisi learnt from Karima

---

[68] See Shams al-Din Muhammad bin 'Abdu al-Rahman al-Sakhawi, *Al-Daw' al-Lami' li-Ahl al-Qarn al-Tasi'*, Beirut, Maktabah al-Hayah, n.d., vol.12; Ahmad bin Ali bin Hajar al-Asqalani, *Al-Durar al-Kaminah fi A'yan al-Mi'ah al-Thaminah*, ed. 'Abd al-Warith Muhammad Ali, Beirut, Dar al-Kutub al-'Ilmiyyah, 1997; Ruth Roded, *Women in Islamic Biographical Collections: From Ibn Sa'd's to Who's Who*, Boulder, Colo.: Lynne Rienner Publishers, 1994, p.68. All cited in Khaled M. Abou El-Fadl, *And God Knows the Soldiers: The Authoritative and Authoritarian in Islamic Discourse*, University Press of America, Inc., Maryland, 2001, p.137.

[69] Ahmad bin Ali bin Hajar Al-Asqalani, *Tahzib al-Tahzib*, Maktabah Da'irah al-Ma'rif al-Nizamiyyah, India, 1326AH, vol.47, p.44, no.2850

[70] Ahmad bin Ali bin Hajar Al-Asqalani, *Tahzeeb al-Tahzeeb*, Matba'ah Da'irah al-Ma'rif al-Nizamiyya, India, 1326AH, vol.42, p.47, no.2841

[71] Imam al-Dhahabi, *Siyar A'alam al-Nubala*, Maktabah al-Shamila 3.13, vol.18, p.234; vol.19, p.120

al-Dimashqiya;[72] Al-Hafiz al-Dimyati learnt from Safiya bint al-Adl;[73] Ibn Salah learnt from Zainab bint Abil Qasim al-Shariya;[74] Abu Tahir Ahmad bin Muhammad al-Silafi studied from Mubaraka bint Abil-Hasan al-Hanbaliyya;[75] Husain bin Abdul Malik al-Khalal studied from Karima bint Abi Sa'd and Aisha bint al-Hasan al-Warkaniyyah;[76] Imam al-Dhahabi learned from Fatimat bint Jauhar;[77] and Ibn Qayyim al-Jawziyyah also studied from Fatimat bint Jauhar.[78]

If some of these women's educational qualifications were to be assessed today in a good university, they

---

[72] Imam al-Dhahabi, *Siyar A'lam al-Nubala*, Maktabah al-Shamila 3.13, vol.23, p.92
[73] Imam al-Dhahabi, *Siyar A'lam al-Nubala*, Maktabah al-Shamila 3.13, vol.23, p.270
[74] Imam al-Dhahabi, *Siyar A'lam al-Nubala*, Maktabah al-Shamila 3.13, vol.23, p.141
[75] Imam al-Dhahabi, *Siyar A'lam al-Nubala*, Maktabah al-Shamila 3.13, vol.21, p.15
[76] Imam al-Dhahabi, *Siyar A'lam al-Nubala*, Maktabah al-Shamila 3.13, vol.17, p.31
[77] Imam al-Dhahabi, *Tazkirah al-Huffaz*, Maktabah al-Shamila 3.13, vol.4, p.1249,
[78] Bakr bin Abdullah Abu Zaid, *Ibn Qayim Al-Jawziya: Hayatuhu Atharuhu wa Mawariduhu*, Dar al-Asima, Riyadh, 1423AH, p.174

would not be ranked as anything less than professors would![79]

Female Companions of the Prophet (p) were also engaged in trading, farming, crafts, teaching, nursing and medicine, and defense, etc. Some, such as Nusaybah bint Ka'b al-Ansariyyah (also known as Umm 'Ammara) were well known for their role in military combat during the Battle of Uhud where she fought beside the Prophet (p) with a sword and shield and killed many of the Makkan soldiers. If in the Sunnah a woman is allowed to fight in military combat, even though she did not have to, then what else can she not learn to do?![80] There were in Islamic History many female scholars of the Qur'an, Hadith, *Fiqh*, female scholars that debated with men, female

---

[79]See also, http://www.muslimheritage.com/article/womens-contribution-classical-islamic-civilisation-science-medicine-and-politics;

[80] For more examples, see http://www.muslimheritage.com/article/womens-contribution-classical-islamic-civilisation-science-medicine-and-politics; http://www.youngmuslimdigest.com/study/02/2015/great-women-islamic-history-forgotten-legacy/; See also the book, *Al-Muhaddithah: The Women Scholars of Islam*, by Mohammad Akram Nadwi – available at https://ia802705.us.archive.org/23/items/AlMuhaddithat/al%20-%20Muhaddithat.pdf

scholars who gave *fatwahs*, reliance of scholars on the *fiqh* of women and their acknowledgement of their scholarship.[81]

The Qur'an and Sunnah have not fixed a limit to the subjects, fields or level of education for either men or women. Each person is required to pursue his or her chosen field of education or training to the highest level possible. Women among the companions of the Prophet (p) were free to study any field of knowledge that is permissible. The Qur'an in fact warns against arbitrarily declaring things as prohibited without the prerequisite evidence from the Sources of Shari'ah. Allah says in the Qur'an (16:116), *"And do not say about what your tongues assert of untruth, "This is lawful and this is unlawful," to invent falsehood about Allah. Indeed, those who invent falsehood about Allah will not succeed."*

As Shari'ah is a complete way of life, the Qur'an and Sunnah recognizes and gives guidance on all aspects

---

[81] See Mohammad Akram Nadwi, *Al-Muhaddithah: The Women Scholars of Islam*, Interface Publications, Oxford, UK, 2007, p.273-290.

of human life – both spiritual or religious (*deen*) and secular or worldly (*dunya*) – in the areas of beliefs or creed(*aqidah*), worship (*ibadah*), morals and conduct (*adab*), social relations and transactions (*mu'amalah*). Based on the Qur'an and Sunnah, there is no subject of study that is permissible for men to study, but prohibited for women and to any level of competence.

The Prophet Muhammad (p) said, "The search for knowledge is an obligation (*faridatun*) upon every Muslim".[82] Muslim scholars have always understood this hadith and many other general statements enjoining Muslims to search and pray for useful knowledge (*'ilman nafi'an*) as applying to both males and females. Useful knowledge could be for the fulfillment of an individual obligation (*fard ayn*) or a collective obligation (*fard kifayah*). Useful knowledge could also be encouraged or recommended (*mustahab*), or it could be merely permissible (*mubah*) depending on how essential it is for bringing benefit (*maslahah*) or preventing harm (*mafsadah*). The Prophet (p) said, *"The best of people are those that*

---

[82] Al-Tirmidhi, Hadith no.74

bring most benefit to the rest of mankind",[83] *"The best of you are the best of you in fulfilling (rights)",*[84] *"The best of you are those who are best to their families, and I am the best of you to my family,"*[85] and *"The best of you are those who feed others and return greetings."*[86] The better the quality and quantity of education and knowledge you have, the more your usefulness and benefit is to yourself, your family, the Muslim Ummah and humanity.

The need for a Muslim society to have female doctors (for female patients and children), female lawyers (for female clients), female policewomen (for female criminals or suspects), female prison wardens, female teachers and lecturers, female customs and immigration officers, security agents, drug detectives, etc. is a social or collective obligation (*fard kifayah*) on the Muslim Ummah and its leadership.

---

[83] Musnad al-Shihab 1234, Kanzul Umal 43065 Albani said the hadith is "hasan" Sahih aljamiu al-Sagir 6662
[84] Ibn Majah :2286
[85] Al-Tirmidhi 3895, Ibn Majah 1977, Tabarani 6145
[86] Abu Ya'la, Musnad Abu Ya'lah Sahih al-Jamu al-Sagir 3318

When a "collective obligation" is not adequately taken care of, it is "upgraded" to an "individual obligation" and it becomes the obligation of every responsible Muslim to find a way to ensure it is adequately fulfilled. We presently do not have sufficient women performing some of these gender-specific *fard kifayah* roles! Consequently, some of these responsibilities become individual obligations (*fard ayn*) which every Muslim (and especially the leadership) must urgently find ways to solve.

In Islamic jurisprudence (*Usul al-fiqh*), whatever is necessary for the fulfillment of a collective social or individual obligation (*fard kifayah* or *fard ayn* respectively) is itself regarded as an obligation (*fard*). The study of medicine at university is therefore an obligation (*fard*) if having doctors is also an obligation (*fard*). So also are the pre-requisite education and subjects in secondary and primary schools regarded as *fard*. The broad and general education to the highest levels for girls and women therefore is not a luxury (*tahsini*) but a necessity (*darurah*) and a religious obligation (*fard*) on the Muslim Ummah.

How then can the basic education of girls or women - which is an obligation (*fard*) - be sacrificed when many Muslims die and many others suffer because of the lack of sufficient competent people – both men and women – in various important professions and essential services?

Generally, seeing a male doctor by an adult female or vice-versa is not permissible (*halal*). It is forbidden (*haram*). However, many jurists have considered it permissible on the grounds that it is a matter of necessity (*darurah*) and also a lesser evil. A state of *darurah* is not meant to be a permanent state or new way of life for Muslims. It is undesirable and meant to be overcome and removed by all means necessary so that Muslim women (and men) can live with dignity and with the full freedom to practice the ideals of their faith.

- According to scholars of hadith, all hadith discouraging women from being taught literacy or knowledge are fabricated.[87]

---

[87] Muhammad Atiyyah Salim, *Tatimmah adwa al-bayan*, Maktabah al-Shamila, 3.13, vol.2, p.252

B. THE LEARNING ENVIRONMENT OF EDUCATIONAL INSTITUTIONS

14. On the Morally Corrupting Environment of Campuses

Educational institutions and campuses are morally corrupting – with alcohol, music, smoking, drugs, immodesty, promiscuity, rape, cultism, etc. - Would it be permissible for Muslim students to attend such institutions?

Not all educational institutions have these vices, crimes and immorality taking place on their campuses. Consequently, this objection only holds for some and not all educational institutions and campuses. Some have these vices taking place in them but not more than what would be found in most public places such as markets, sports fields, parks, road side, houses, shopping centres, towns, villages and even some Islamic schools (or *madrasas*)!

Actions and matters are judged by their main purposes. The main purpose of a market is to create a place where buying and selling can take place. The fact that cheating, stealing and lying, etc. takes place there does not mean it is not a market or that it is haram for Muslims to go there. The same would apply to other places such as hotels, restaurants, offices, prisons, hospitals, farms, buses, trains, 'Eid grounds, mosques and even around the Ka'bah (or Masjid al-Haram) in Makkah where Muslims go for Hajj and Umrah. Just because some people do wrong and immoral things in these places does not make them prohibited for Muslims, nor does it mean that they are no more meant for their original purposes.

People have weaknesses and so do places. The concern is whether the harm is the same as or exceeds the benefit of the place. Also, whether there are ways of effectively reducing if not eliminating the harm, or at least protecting innocent persons from the influence of the harm or evil.

Muslims are expected to move away from places that are evil only if they cannot stop it or change it, and if they fear that they cannot resist the influence of such places.

The immorality, corruption and evil of Makkah during the *Jahiliyyah* period were greater than that of most places today. Yet, the Prophet (p) and his companions did not migrate (do *hijrah*) until after they were persecuted and their survival was actually threatened. The Sunnah of the Prophet was not to run away from evil, but to unite and find effective ways of resisting and changing it for the better. "*Wa qul ja'al haq, wa zahaqal batil...*" – "*Say, truth has come, and falsehood has perished...*" (Qur'an 17:81)

If one however fears for himself, and considers the temptation too strong for him or her to handle, then it may be advisable for him or her to change to a better environment. Nevertheless, one should not condemn or judge those who stay back to try to change things for themselves and others to come.

The Qur'an and Sunnah have given many guidelines for Muslims on how to deal with immoral and evil temptations and situations. "*Whoever sees something *wrong, let him change it with his hand; and if he can't, then with his tongue; and if he can't, then with his heart..."*[88]

When you can't change wrong or evil, you should still try to protect yourself and others from its influence. Depending on the form of corrupting influence, Muslims may be advised to lower their gaze and guard their modesty; warn people about the evil and share ways of avoiding or resisting or controlling it; convince wrongdoers of the wrongness of their ways; expose those insistent on supporting or doing injustice and wrong; use the law where possible to prevent or sanction law-breakers; walk away from wrongdoing if you can't change it; advise people to avoid bad friendships/relations; avoid negatively influencing contexts; focus on your priorities and avoid distractions; support positive change activities; build more networks with others who also feel change is needed; do your best, keep trying and never give up; forgive people for their mistakes, pray for them and give them another chance; think well of people, find

---

[88] *Sahih Muslim*, no.79, Dar Ihya Turath al-Arabi, Beirut

excuses for them and give them the benefit of doubt; stand for justice and tell the truth; take studies seriously, build networks and become more influential; keep learning and listen to good scholars; be creative in finding and trying new approaches to change; learn from the experience of others; learn to speak convincingly and peacefully to key stakeholders and those in authority; work towards better policies and laws, and their enforcement; do your best, however little; complain less and act more; make good friends and consult more; be patient with others and the often natural and gradual pace of effective and sustainable long-term change; count your blessings and be grateful for your situation and appreciate the efforts of those who went before (it could have been much worse!); pray often and never give up on Allah's mercy and support; work on the purification of your heart; be humble, curious, sincere and committed to change; have faith that Allah's way is the best; etc. *"Allah is with those who patiently persevere"* (Qur'an 2:153); *"Invite all to the way of your Lord, with wisdom and beautiful exhortation, and argue with them in the ways that are best and most gracious"*

(Qur'an 16:125); *"When you meet the ignorant, speak peace to them"* (Qur'an 25:63) ; The Prophet (p) said, *"A believer who mixes with people and perseveres in spite of their harm is better than the one who does not…."*

So, while various environments such as schools, markets, communities, and other organizations and institutions may have various levels of evil and corruption in them, good Muslims must not leave these places to be fully under the control of immoral people. They must effectively resist evil and struggle towards changing things for the better in the long term as did the Prophet (p) and his companions, and all the great scholars.

Educational reforms at all levels are made by experts of the highest qualifications and political or administrative authority, which requires the study of Education, Management, Public Administration, Law, etc. This benefit can be seen from the Nigerian experience and that of many countries with both private and public schools. A Muslim should study to the highest level and work with the intention of bringing positive reform to any and all sectors of the society that needs improvement, however small that change may be. This role is a collective religious obligation (*fard kifayah*) upon Muslims. Failure to become leaders or positively influence the leadership in any aspect of life exposes Muslims to discrimination and bigoted policies of others which in turn creates resentment, frustration and interfaith tension.

15. On Co-education being Immoral and Un-Islamic

Some have argued that co-education leads to immorality and lewdness. Will this not be a legitimate reason for Islamic Law to prohibit Muslims from attending such schools?

When we say "co-education" is un-Islamic, do we mean that it is prohibited (*haram*) according to the Qur'an and Sunnah for males and females to be in the same place, compound or school environment? Or do we mean it is prohibited (*haram*) for males and females to be in the same building and classroom? Or do we mean it is prohibited (*haram*) for them to be seated beside each other in a classroom even if they have no physical contact with each other?

While there may be many practical, cultural and beneficial reasons for segregating male and female students in a school, to claim that Islamic law prohibits (as *haram*) anything, requires clear explicit evidence from the authoritative texts of the Qur'an and Sunnah.

Islamic law has never prohibited Muslim males and females from getting together in the same place for anything that is beneficial and not prohibited. Since the time of the Prophet (p) and his companions, men and women were not prohibited from working in and visiting the same markets, worshipping in the same *'Eid* prayer ground, and also during Hajj and Umrah, etc. They were also not prohibited from being in the same building such as a mosque or courtroom.

Several ahadith in *Sahih al-Bukhari* and *Muslim*, for instance, narrate the marriage of Umm Usaid and Abu Usaid Al-Sa'adī at the time of the Prophet (p), where the bride (Umm Usaid) was serving male guests including the Prophet (p).[89] With reference to this instance, Ibn Hajr al-Asqalani comments:

> "From this hadith, we conclude that a woman is permitted to serve her husband and his male visitors, just as the husband is permitted to serve his wife. It is evident that her serving the visitors is allowed only if there is no fear of temptation

---

[89] See for example, *Sahih al-Bukhari*, vol.7, nos.111-112, 495, 502 in *Alim 6.0*

and if she is properly dressed; if the wife is not properly dressed (as is the case with a majority of women in our time) her appearing in front of men is *haram*.[90]

This hadith makes it clear that males and female who are together or in each other's proximity for reasons that are not immoral are permitted to interact so long as they respect Islamic codes of conduct and behavior.

While coeducation or males and females being in the same school or classroom may be discouraged for various other reasons, it is not prohibited (*haram*) byany explicit teachings of the Qur'an and Sunnah, nor based on the practice of the Prophet's Companions.

What is prohibited is immoral behavior anywhere, whether in the school, mosque, market, home or elsewhere. The Qur'an warns, "*Do not go near illicit sexual relations (zina)...*" (Qur'an 17:32) It is up to concerned Muslim individuals, parents' and students'

---

[90] Cited in Sheikh Yusuf al-Qaradawi's discussion on this topic in *The Lawful and the Prohibited in Islam* (London: Al-Birr Foundation, 2003), p.152

associations (such as the Muslim Students' Society of Nigeria – MSSN), and the leadership or administration of the relevant institutions and programmes to consider how best to effectively prevent and/or check specific unacceptable immoral or unethical behavior.

Depending on the authority of each stakeholder, educational institutions could consider better guidance and counseling for students, better teaching of ethics and morals for students and teachers, better public dressing and behavior, more mosque activities (*da'wah, nasihah, ta'lim*, etc.), extra lessons, better students' welfare and security, more effective policies and laws prohibiting alcohol and drugs on campuses, better consultation with students on how best to tackle specific challenges, more appropriate and effective sanctions for misbehavior, recruitment of better role models among staff, etc.

However, while no environment will be completely free of vices and corrupt individuals, the existence of coeducational institutions cannot and should not be a reason for Muslims to deny themselves or others the benefit of better education and the opportunities for change that come with it, which is actually the primary purpose for which these institutions were established. Concerned Muslims should acquire the necessary qualifications and authority to more effectively enjoin what is right and forbid wrong whether as students, staff, parents, or as community leaders, etc.

While co-educational institutions may be Islamically acceptable for the reasons given above, some parents may still feel their children would do better and be safer in single-sex schools meant for only boys or only girls. This is important to encourage, as globally, girls in particular appear to do better academically in only-girls schools than they do in mixed or co-educational institutions since there is naturally less sexual misbehavior in such schools.

16. Schools and the Islamic Dress Code

Some schools prohibit Muslim girls from dressing in a manner that is compliant with Islamic teachings. Is it prohibited for Muslim girls to attend such schools?

Islamic teaching prescribes a compulsory minimum dress code for both boys and girls when they reach puberty. For boys it is from the navel to the knees, while for girls it is the whole body with the exception of the face and hands. This is the understanding of the majority of Muslim scholars and schools of law (*madhahib*). A school uniform for that age group should therefore respect this religious requirement. This is the case in many schools where there is adequate respect for religious freedom and expression.

In many predominantly Muslim states in Nigeria, boys and girls are able to wear a version of the school uniform that is respectful of Islamic requirements. The argument that girls should not go to school because *hijab* is a religious obligation that is prohibited by schools, cannot therefore be used to prevent girls from pursuing their education in those schools that are tolerant or respectful of the *hijab*.

In some places however, the only quality schools for children are private non-Muslim schools that are not sufficiently respectful or sensitive to the dressing needs of especially Muslim women. Sometimes, there are government schools where the administration does not allow Muslim girls to wear Islamically compliant uniforms.

One of the lessons we learn from the Sunnah of the Prophet (p) is to have a sense of priority when faced with such dilemmas and challenges. During the well-known Treaty of Hudaibiyyah for example, the Prophet (p) had to make a choice between a long-term benefit of a peace treaty with the Pagan Quraysh, and the short-term legitimate rights and need of movement of oppressed Muslims from Makkah to Madinah. The Prophet (p) regarded the long-term benefits of peace as a priority over the short-term needs. Most of the Prophet's (p) companions were unhappy about the Prophet's (p) decision, as they were more concerned about the dignity of Islam and the clear needs of the oppressed Muslims. The Prophet's (p) choice for long-term peace however allowed Muslims to take advantage of the period of peace to build better relations with others, enlighten more people about the true message of Islam and increase in the number of Muslims and their influence. When eventually the Pagan Quraish broke the treaty, the Muslims had enough strength and influence to get both long-term peace, security and the full rights of movement for Muslims who were now no longer oppressed. From this and many other cases in the Sunnah, scholars conclude that it is permissible to sacrifice or forgo a short-term benefit for a much longer-term advantage.

Muslim scholars have picked many pieces of wisdom from the methodology of change taught by the Qur'an and Sunnah, and have converted these into short memorable statements or "legal maxims" (*qawa'id*) to guide Muslims when faced with various dilemmas in new context which specific texts may not have directly addressed. Some of these maxims include:

- "A greater harm can be eliminated by means of a lesser harm." (*Yuzal ad-darar al-ashadd bi al-darar al-akhaff*).

- "We choose the better of two beneficial alternatives, and the lesser of the two evils when there is a choice." (*Nakhtar a'la al-maslahatain, wa akhaff al-mafsdatain inda al-tazahum*)

- "A specific harm is tolerated in order to prevent a more general one." (*Yutahammal al-darar al-khaas li-daf' al-darar al 'am*).

- "Whatever is a prerequisite or necessity for an obligation (*wajib*) is itself regarded as an obligation (*wajib*)." (*Ma la yatimm al-wajib illabihi fahuwa wajib*).

- "To repel a public damage, a private damage is preferred". (*Al-darar al-'am li daf'al-darar al-khas*)[91]

---

[91] Ali bin Na'if al-Shuhud, *Al-Khulasa fi Fiqh al-Aqalliyyah*, Maktabah al-Shamila 3.13, vol.7, p.48

The Muslim Ummah has learnt many lessons in survival, growth and societal reform over the centuries in many societies. There are many institutions in many societies – schools, universities, hospitals, law firms, government offices, administrative positions, security services, media organizations, etc. – that formerly did not allow women to wear any Islamically-compliant dressing (*hijab*). However, Muslim sisters sacrificed the short-term advantage of the dignity of the *hijab* for the long-term advantage of getting a better education, greater authority and influence with the intention of ultimately reforming the system. And in the long-run, with Allah's support, these now influential women (and men) have been able to influence reforms in long-standing discriminatory policies that now accommodate and respect Islamically-compliant dress codes and many other needs of Muslim men and women related to food, drink, clothing, finance, laws, culture, etc. The early sacrifices of those Muslim women – similar to those done by many early Muslims - have resulted in a present situation where all women are now free to dress with dignity according to the dictates of their faith and have much greater religious freedoms.

While this approach may take time, hard work, sacrifices, disappointments, patience and perseverance, it so far appears the most assured route for positive change that the Ummah has used, and the real test of sincerity of purpose and faith in the methodology of the Sunnah. To decide not to attend educational or professional institutions because they are presently not tolerant of any form of *hijab* is to lose the time-tested long-term benefits that come with gradual but ultimate reform. You may win the "battle" for yourself to dress appropriately, but probably also lose the "war" for the Ummah and posterity.

As some wise scholars say, "In life you do not get what you deserve. You get what you can negotiate and work for!" Most societies would usually not change their laws and policies just to suit Muslim needs. It is the responsibility of Muslims to find the most effective ways of gaining respect and influence, and better means of communicating and securing their needs sustainably and for the long term.

There is however the need for more qualified Muslims in the field of Law and Human Rights who are competent enough to take legal action against bigots, extremists and others who would want to deny Muslims (or anyone else) of their legally protected religious freedoms. This also calls for Muslims to pursue conventional education to the highest level possible.

Better interfaith relations can also play an important role in reducing the use of religious sentiments and bigotry by some to discriminate against and deny others their constitutional rights and religious freedom, which at the same time do not trample on the rights and freedom of others.

The importance of a good education for Muslim women (and men) and the opportunities for reform of society and the progress of Islam that come with it are too valuable to be sacrificed for short-term benefits of the various reason and excuses presented for avoiding such an education. These long-term benefits affect many rights of Muslim women in the family and society, *da'wah* to non-Muslims, health of women, poverty alleviation, morality, drugs, and most social problems that require competent Muslims women to attend to them.

17. Wearing the Face-veil (*Niqab*) in School

Some schools allow their Muslims girls to wear uniforms that are compliant with Islamic *hijab* requirements, but they do not permit the wearing of the *niqab* (the face-veil). Is it permissible for Muslim girls who regard wearing the *niqab* as obligatory to abandon their studies or regard attending such schools as prohibited?

Not all schools prevent hijab or *niqab*. The argument that girls should not go to school because *hijab* or *niqab* is a religious obligation but prohibited by schools, cannot therefore be used to prevent girls from pursuing their education in schools that are tolerant or respectful of the *hijab* and/or *niqab*.

The arguments presented earlier (question No.16) are important for some Muslim women to consider – in accordance with the methodology of the Sunnah – the choice of the lesser evil - sacrificing of the wearing of *niqab* in the short-term, for the longer term and more permanent benefit of many more women in the future being able to wear the *niqab*, also applies to this question.

For most scholars and schools of law (*madhahib*), the *niqab* is not compulsory (*fard/wajib*) for Muslim women. It is at most recommended (*mustahab*).[92] The long benefits to the Ummah as a whole of a sincere Muslim sister's education are more valuable than the wearing of a recommended *niqab*. A Muslim girl should therefore not abandon her studies and its benefits simply because she is not allowed to wear a *niqab*.

In Islamic jurisprudence, even those scholars who insist that the *niqab* is compulsory agree that a Muslim woman is allowed to unveil her *niqab* in court for identification.[93] If therefore the unveiling of the *niqab* is required for security or examination identification,

---

[92] This is based on a number of authentic hadith such as this one: Qatadah narrated that the Prophet (pbuh) said, "*When a young lady begins to menstruate, it is not proper that anything should be seen of her except her face and hands.*" (Abu Dawud). For further discussion on this subject, see Nasir al-Din al-Albani, *Jilbab Al-Mar'ah Al-Muslimah fi al- Kitab wa al-Sunnah,* Beirut: Al-Maktab al-Islamiyyah, 1994, pp.57-59.

[93] Ministry of Awqaf and Religious Affairs, *al-Mawsu'ah al-Fiqhiyyah al-Kuwaitiyyah,* Dar al-Salasil, 1427AH, vol.4, p.316

to prevent or reduce fraud, then the greater good (*maslahah*) and concern for the society should prevail. Even if wearing the *niqab* was regarded as *wajib*, the existence of the necessity (*darurah* or *haajah*) of security concerns for a society would permit its removal or disuse. The leadership of an institution is permitted in Shari'ah to "block means" to harm (*sadd al-dhara'i*), and forbid the use of *niqab* if there is a real fear for the security and safety of others, and there are no other effective alternative measures.

The existence of some girls-only schools however reduces or removes the need for wearing the *niqab*, and those who would like to insist on *niqab* could consider transferring to such schools if faced with school options that are intolerant of *niqab*.

It is necessary that there were more female security personnel and examination invigilators to inspect and verify the identity of *niqab*-wearing women. It naturally also implies the need for more educated Muslim female professionals in security services.

18. On Serving the Nation instead of Serving Only Allah

Some Muslims believe that any form of "national service" such as the National Youth Service Corps (NYSC) is an act of disbelief (*Kufr*), because it is a form of serving the nation instead of serving Allah, the only One Who should be served. (It should also be noted that in Hausa language, "national service" is translated as "bautan kasa" which literally means "worshipping the nation"). Is it permissible for a Muslim to serve others or his nation while also serving Allah?

The argument in the above question seems to assume that serving one's nation, family, guests, etc. is somehow contradictory to serving Allah; that one cannot serve one's parents if only Allah should be served. It neglects that fact that serving Allah actually requires us to serve His creation in accordance with His guidance in the Qur'an and Sunnah.

Allah says in the Qur'an, "*I have not created jinn and men for any other purpose than for them to serve Me*". (Qur'an 51:56)

The word translated as "serve" (*ibadah*) in the verse above is, when used for Allah, also understood to mean worship in the sense of directing devotion and religious rituals towards Allah alone. When applied to Allah, it means that we do not serve or submit to the will of any creature in a way that implies disobedience to Allah as taught by the Prophet (p). When we are described as servants of Allah, it means Allah is our ultimate Master and we do not serve any other in a way that contradicts our pledge (or *shahadah*) to Allah.

It does not literally mean that there are no more "servants" in peoples' homes, and no more "masters" of the house (*Rabb al-Bait*). It also does not mean a Muslim cannot "serve" others such as "serving" his/her guests, parents, family, stranger, neighbours, community, society, nation, the Ummah or humanity or even serving the needs of other creatures. It does not mean that people cannot also be civil "servants" or part of a group of youth "serving" the nation (i.e. the National Youth Service Corps – NYSC). In fact these and many other forms of showing compassion and being useful to others or social service are all different ways of serving Allah.

What is prohibited for a Muslim is to serve others in ways or for purposes that contradict the teachings of Islam and which are therefore forms of disobedience to Allah.

The various ways of "serving" Allah therefore are actually fulfilled through selflessly serving His creation by following His guidance. We are taught to serve Allah through serving others. The Prophet (p) said, "The best among you are those who are most useful to others"[94]. In reality, Allah is in no need of our service and worship, as He is independent of these. A careful study of all religious and mundane teachings of Islam shows that they are all aimed at benefiting humanity (*maslahah*) or removing harm and evil

---

[94] Abu Bakr Ahmad bin Husain al-Baihaqi, *Shu'ab al-Iman*, Dar al-Kutub al-Ilmiyyah, Beirut, 1410AH, vol.6, p.117, hadith no.7658; Daraqutni

(*mafsadah*) in this life and the next. Therefore, selfless service to Allah's creation is also regarded as serving Allah.

The Prophet (p) said, *"Whoever does not show gratitude to people has not shown gratitude to Allah"*[95]; *"Show mercy to those on earth and He who is in heaven will show mercy to you"*[96]; In a long "divine" (*qudsi*) hadith, Allah, on the Day of Judgment describes Himself as having been "hungry", "thirsty" and "sick" and was not tended to by the Believer. When the Believer asks how it could be possible for Allah the Almighty to be "hungry", "thirsty" and "sick", Allah responds by saying "My servant was hungry, …thirsty and …sick, and you did not tend to him."[97] Aisha was asked about what the Prophet (p) did while he was at home, and she said, "He served his

---

[95] Muhammad bin Ismail al-Bukhari, *al-Adab al-Mufrad*, Dar al-Bashair al-Islamiyya, Beirut, 1989, p.85, hadith no.218; Sulaiman bin Abu Dawud, *Sunan Abi Dawud*, Dar al-Kitab al-Araby, Beirut, vol.4, p.403, hadith no.4813

[96] Al-Tirmidhi, 1924; *Musnad Imam Ahmad*, 6494; Abu Bakar Ahmad bin al-Husain bin Ali bin Musa al-Baihaqi, *al-Sunan al-Kubra*, Maktabat Dar al-Baz, Makkah, 1994, vol.9, p.41, hadith no.17683

[97] *Sahih Muslim*, 6721.

family".[98] These hadiths clearly show that serving and tending to the legitimate needs of Allah's creation are an important way of serving Allah.

The Hausa translation of "National Service" as "*bautan kasa*" (literally, "worshipping the land") does not change the real and accepted meaning of the term as a form of service. Even though the word "*bauta*" also means worship in the devotional sense, no educated Hausa person uses the word to literally mean that people are worshipping the nation in the same sense as they worship or show devotion to Allah.

Also, while some have criticized the immoral and unethical activities of some of the Service Corp members as also found within all professions (Islamiyyah and other teachers, lecturers, *mallams*, police, mechanics, rural farmers, cattle herdsmen, etc.), this still does not constitute disbelief (*kufr*), nor is it sufficient to make such responsibilities *haram* for everyone else.

---

[98] *Sahih al-Bukhari*, 676; *Musnad Ahmad*, 24226

Wrongdoing by corps members only underscores the critical importance of more efforts by concerned Muslims and all stakeholders to find legitimate and effective ways of enjoining right and forbidding wrong.

The NYSC members, especially through the Muslim Corpers' Association of Nigeria (MCAN), have also done a lot of good in spreading a better understanding of Islam, building community and offering many humanitarian and other services to various distant communities.

19. The National Anthem and Pledge and a Muslim's *Shahadah*

Some Muslims regard the National Pledge and National Anthem as a form of glorifying the nation instead of glorifying only Allah. The Nigerian national pledge and anthem ask citizens "...to be faithful, loyal and honest", "to serve Nigeria with all my strength...", "to serve our fatherland...", etc. Such loyalty and service is understood to be due only to God. Those who recite these pledges and anthems – such as students, civil servants, armed forces, media houses, etc. - are regarded as disbelievers (*Kuffar*). Are Muslims permitted to recite national pledges and anthems?

The answer to this question is similar to No.18: On Serving the Nation instead of serving only Allah.

Any form of service to the best of one's ability ("with all my strength") towards the family, neighbours and others which does not imply any disobedience to Allah is not just permissible (*halal*) but even encouraged (*mustahab*) in Islamic law. The provision of essential services to the community and nation are in fact regarded in Islam as a collective social obligation (*fardkifayah*) and must be performed.

The national pledge is simply a promise to be faithful, loyal and honest in giving service to the people of Nigeria - through enjoining right and forbidding wrong - that is *halal*. Being faithful, loyal and honest, along with other virtues are essential for any true believer. The Prophet (p) instructed Muslims and their leadership to always honour and stand by the agreements they make: "*Al Muslimu inda shurutihim!*" ("Muslims are bound by the conditions they accept"), and all believers are characterized in the Qur'an as those "*who are faithful to their trusts and to their pledges*" (Qur'an 23:8).

The national pledge does not imply that one cannot give service to other creatures or to the rest of Africa or humanity. The pledge also ends with a prayer - "So help me God!" It therefore recognizes and honours God, and makes it clear that the pledge/promise requires God's blessing and support.

Serving Allah and the country are not automatically mutually exclusive. Serving a part of or all humanity is a way of serving God, with God's assistance. True faith (*iman*) is in serving others – family, neighbours, the community and nation, etc.

The second stanza or part of the National Pledge is actually a supplication (*du'a*) to Allah for guidance and for "a nation where peace and justice shall reign". As it is a supplication or request (*du'a*) to Allah and not a "ritual prayer" (*salah*), it can be said in any language, facing any direction and done at any time, without ablution (*wudu*). The fact also that there are better-structured and more comprehensive supplications within the Islamic tradition does not make the pledge bad or even discouraged.

The national anthem is a motivational song that encourages people "to serve …with love and strength and faith" and a hope for a "nation bound in freedom, peace and unity". The anthem is made up of good words, and does not contradict Qur'an and Sunnah. Such noble songs or poetry especially when unaccompanied with musical instruments are decent and permissible (*halal*).[99] Where they are accompanied by musical instruments, there will be the same differences of opinions among the scholars (such as Ibn Hazm, Al-Shawkani, Al-Qaradawi, and others) as discussed earlier on in No.12: On Attending Institutions that Teach Subjects that are *Haram*. The differences of opinion among distinguished scholars should not be a basis for disunity and the breaking of brotherhood.

The teaching or rehearsing of the National Anthem or Pledge is therefore not a basis for avoiding or discouraging anyone from going to school or pursuing education.

---

[99] Wahbah al-Zuhayli, *al-Fiqh al-Islami wa Adillatuhu*, Dar al-Fikr, Damascus, vol.4, p.214

20. Standing up in Respect for Other than Allah is Un-Islamic

The Prophet (p) prohibited people from standing up out of respect for him. Many schools teach their students to stand up in respect for the teacher upon entering the classroom. Is standing up for a teacher (or anyone else) prohibited in Islamic law? Does this practice make attending schools or classes where such is done also prohibited for Muslims?

There are a number of hadith quoted to justify the prohibition of standing up in respect for others:

- Anas reported that when they saw the Prophet (p) *"they did not stand up because they knew of his dislike for that."*[100]

- Anas also reported that the Prophet (p) said, *"Those before you have been ruined by the fact

---

[100] Al-Tirmidhi 2754

that they have glorified their kings by standing up as their kings sit down."[101]

- Jabir is reported to have said, *"You were about to do as the Persians and Byzantines do. They stand while their kings sit down. Do not do that!"*[102]

- When Abdullah bin Zubayr and Ibn Safwan stood up for Mu'awiyya, he said, *"Sit down, for I heard the Prophet (p) say, 'Let he who is pleased by people standing up before him, await his place in Hell'."*[103]

- When Mu'adh bin Jabal in imitation of the people of Sham prostrated before the Prophet (p), the Prophet (p) then said, *"Were I to have commanded anyone to prostrate to anyone, I would have commanded the wife to prostrate*

---

[101] Bukhari, *Adab al-Mufrad*, 202.
[102] Cited in Khaled M. Abou El-Fadl, *And God Knows the Soldiers: The Authoritative and Authoritarian in Islamic Discourse*, University Press of America, Inc., Maryland, 2001, p.49. (Hereinafter referenced as El-Fadl, 2001)
[103] Abu Dawud 5231, Tirmidhi 2755

to her husband."[104] This hadith is used by some as the basis for an analogy (*qiyas*) with standing up.

The hadiths above clearly demonstrates that the Prophet (p) took issue with people standing up before him, and that a Muslims should not desire others to stand up out of respect for him or her. It also makes it clear that this is also out of fear that this could lead to over-respect and veneration as it happened in the past. In a similar vein, the Prophet (p) is reported to also have said "Do not venerate me" (*"la tatruni"*).[105]

Other authentic hadiths however also clearly show that the Prophet (p) himself did stand up out of respect for others and even encouraged some of his companions to do the same, especially where there was no fear that this would lead to conceit or undue veneration.

---

[104] Al-Tirmidhi 1159, Abu Dawud 2140, Musnad Ahmad 19422
[105] Ahmad ibn Hajar al-Asqalani, *Fath al-Bari fi Sharh al-Bukhari*, Dar al-Fikr, Beirut, 1993, 12:322. Cited El-Fadl, 2001, p.49. Based on some of these, Imam Malik ruled that a woman may not remain standing before her husband. (Ibn Hajar, *Fath al-Bari*, 1993, 12:319, cited in El-Fadl, 2001, p.56)

- According to a number of companions, the Prophet (p) commanded some of the *Ansar* (helpers) to "Stand up for your master" ("*qumu ila sayyidikim*") who was Sa'ad bin Mu'adh.[106]

- Abu Hurayrah reports that when the Prophet (p) would stand up to leave, the companions would stand up and remain standing until he left the mosque.[107]

- The Prophet (p) stood up during a Jewish funeral procession for a dead Jew and the reason given by the Prophet (p) for his action when he was asked, was "But is she not a soul?"[108]

---

[106] Al-Baihaqi, *Al-Sunan al-Kubrah*, hadith no. 18648; Abu Dawud, *Sunan Abu Dawud*, Hadith no5217; al-Nasa'I, *Al-Sunan Al-Kubrah*, hadith no. 8222; Al-Bukhari, *Sahih al-Bukhari*, hadith no. 3043, 4121 & 6282; Muslim, *Sahih Muslim*, hadith no. 4695

[107] Abu Dawud, 110

[108] Al- Tirmidhi 3174, an-Nasa'i 1927, Abu Dawud 3174, Ahmad 14591

- The Prophet (p) stood up to receive and greet his daughter Fatima[109], Ikrima bin Abi Jahl or the Prophet's (p) suckling brother.[110]

Based on all these seemingly contradictory but authentic hadith narrations, some scholars such as Ibn Qayyim and Ibn Hajar have concluded that it is prohibited to stand up as a show of respect.[111] Others such as Al-Nawawi, Al-Baghawi, Al-Ghazali and al-Baihaqi have concluded that it is permissible to stand up out of compassion or respect.[112] Others such as Al-'aini[113] and Ibn Hajar al-Asqalani[114] conclude that there is no definite conclusion or resolution among scholars on the issue of standing because of their disagreements. They both (along with others)

---

[109] Sahih Muslim *6467*
[110] Ibn Hajar al-Asqalani, *Fath al-Bari*, 1993, 12:321. See also al-Bukhari, *Al-Adaba al-Mufrad*, 201-2. Cited El-Fadl, 2001, p.57
[111] Ibn Hajar al-Asqalani, *Fath al-Bari*, 1993, 12:320. This view is also held by Al-Albani in his *Silsilah al-Ahadith al-Da'ifah*, 3:637-8. Cited in El-Fadl, 2001, p.59.
[112] Husain bin Mas'ud al-Baghawi, *Sharh al-Sunnah*, Beirut, Dar al-Fikr, 1994, 7:213; Ibn Hajar al-Asqalani, *Fath al-Bari*, 1993, 12:320, 323. Cited in El-Fadl, 2001, p.59
[113] Badr al-Din Mahmud bin Ahmad al-'aini, *'Umdah al-Qari bi Sharh Sahih al-Bukhari*, Beirut, Dar al-Firk, n.d., 11:251. Cited in El-Fadl, 2001, p.58
[114] Ibn Hajar al-Asqalani, *Fath al-Bari*, 1993, 12:317.

however said that it is recommended to stand up for a leader, a just ruler (*imam*), an elder, or a knowledgeable person.[115]

In reconciling the various hadiths on this issue, some of these scholars, including al-Tabari and al-Nawawi, make a subtle but important distinction between a proud or egotistical desire for others to stand up for oneself (which is prohibited based on some of these hadiths) and standing up for others out of one's own humility, modesty and respect for them (which is permissible based on the other hadith).[116] Al-Tabari argues therefore that it all depends on the intention – Is it promoting arrogance and conceit, or merely showing of respect?[117]

Some other scholars try to reconcile these hadiths by concluding that there are different occasions and consequences of standing up presented in all the

---

[115] Husayn bin Mas'ud al-Baghawi, *Sharh al-Sunnah*, Beirut, Dar al-Fikr, 1994, 7:213; Ibn Hajar al-Asqalani, *Fath al-Bari*, 1993, 12:320, 323. Cited in El-Fadl, 2001, p.59

[116] Ibn Hajar al-Asqalani, *Fath al-Bari*, 1993, 12:318, 322. Cited in El-Fadl, 2001, p.59.

[117] Ibn Hajar al-Asqalani, *Fath al-Bari*, 1993, 12:320. Cited in El-Fadl, 2001, p.59

relevant hadith, and depending on these, standing up as a show of respect could be prohibited (*haram*), discouraged (*discouraged*), merely permissible (*mubah*) or even encouraged (*mustahab*). According to Ibn Rushd, standing up is of four types:[118]

1. It is prohibited for one to arrogantly and self-conceitedly want others to stand up in his presence.

2. It is reprehensible to stand up to one who is not conceited or arrogant, but of whom it is feared that he or she will become conceited or arrogant when people stand up in his or her presence.

3. It is permissible to stand up as a sign of respect before someone who you do not fear will become arrogant.

4. It is recommended that one stand up to greet someone who arrives after travelling.

---

[118]Ibn Hajar al-Asqalani, *Fath al-Bari*, 1993, 12:320; Cited in El-Fadl, 2001, p.59. See also Muhammad bin Salih al-Uthaimin, *Sharh Riyadh al-Salihin*, al-Maktabah al-Shamilah 13.13, vol.1, p.59

Scholars such as Ibn Abd al-Salam and Ibn Hajar al-Asqalani however add that if the failure to stand up will result in insult or create a *mafsada* (corruption or harm) then it becomes forbidden not to stand up.[119] Ibn Hajar al-Haitami says that standing up becomes recommended, if not mandatory, if it is in order to achieve social harmony and to avoid unnecessary conflicts.[120] Al-Shatibi states that the custom of standing up out of respect to greet someone is consistent with the Shari'ah, and it is lawful. He asserts that under the Caliph Umar bin Abdul Aziz, it had become an established practice. This established practice, he argues, was consistent with the precedent set by the Prophet (p) because the Prophet (p) rose to greet his cousin Ja'far.[121]

The Prophet (p) said, "*He is not of us who does not respect our elders, nor show compassion towards our*

---

[119] Ibn Hajar al-Asqalani, *Fath al-Bari*, 1993, 12:323. Cited in El-Fadl, 2001, p.59.
[120] Ibn Hajar al-Haitami, *Al-Fatwahs al-Kubra al-Fiqhiyyah*, Beirut, Dar al-Kutub al-'Ilmiyyah, 1983, 4:247-8. Cited in El-Fadl, 2001, p.58
[121] Ibrahim bin Musa al-Shatibi, *Al-Muwafaqat fi Usul al-Shari'ah*, ed. 'Abdullah Darraz, Cairo, Dar al-Fikr al-'Arab, n.d., 3:64-65. Cited in El-Fadl, 2001, p.60

young ones".¹²² Those who regard it as permissible or even encouraged for a Muslim to stand up out of humility, compassion and respect for others regard it therefore as permissible and even necessary for children or students to be taught such gestures of respect, modesty and humility in school, and especially towards teachers, elders, leaders and parents. The natural challenge and responsibility is for the individual teacher, leader or parent, etc., not to allow himself or herself gradually develop a sense of arrogance, pride and an inner desire from such displays of humility or respect by others.

The fact however still remains that distinguished scholars have and will continue to differ on this issue.¹²³ According to Sufyan At-Thawri,¹²⁴ *"If you see a man doing something over which there is difference of opinion among scholars, and which you believe to*

---

¹²²Bukhari, *Al-Adab al-Mufrad*, 358; *Sunan al-Tirmidhi*, 1919
¹²³For further reading on the issue of standing up for others, and in addition to references already cited above, see also Hasan Ayyub, *Al-Suluk al-Ijtima'i fi al-Islam,* Dar al-Buhuth al-'Ilmiyyah, Cairo, 1979, p.324-332.
¹²⁴ He was also called the *Amirul Mu'minim fil Hadith* ("Leader of the Believer in Hadith") and was among the greatest scholars of the successors (*tabi'un*) of the companions of the Prophet (pbuh).

be forbidden, you should not forbid him from doing it."[125]

Such issues upon which scholars differ (*khilaf*) - and there are many others – cannot and should not be a basis for abandoning education or a school; nor is it a valid basis for attributing the sin of *shirk* or of declaring *kufr*.

It is narrated from Ibn Umar that the Prophet (p) said: *"When a man calls his brother an unbeliever (kafir), it returns (at least) to one of them."*[126] In other words, if you call a person a *kafir*, when he is not, then Allah will regard you as a *kafir*!

---

[125] Quoted in Abdal Hakim Murad, *Understanding the Four Madhahib*, Cambridge: Muslim Academic Trust, 1999, p.13
[126] *Ahmad*, 4687; *Al-Bukhari*, 6103, *Muwatta' Malik*, 3606; *Muslim*, 224

21. Saluting the Flag as similar to Reverence and Worship of an Idol

Some Muslims understand the act of saluting a flag or a superior officer to be similar to an act of reverence, veneration and worship, and therefore regard it as an act of polytheism (*shirk*) and disbelief (*kufr*). Some also regard the salute gesture as similar to the raising of the hands in prayer (*salah*), except that it is done with only one hand. Would saluting a flag or a superior officer be regarded as an act of *kufr* in Islamic Law?

There is no textually based prohibition of the gesture of saluting anyone or anything in the Qur'an or Sunnah of the Prophet Muhammad (p). Allah reminds us in Qur'an (16:116), *"And do not say about what your tongues assert of untruth, "This is lawful and this is unlawful," to invent falsehood about Allah. Indeed, those who invent falsehood about Allah will not succeed."*

The analogy that implies similarity of salutation (to a flag) to prostration (*sujud*) or raising of the hands (in *takbirah Ihram*) in prayer (*salah*) is logically problematic. It implies that any gesture that is in any way similar to a posture done in prayer (*salah*) - such as standing, sitting, turning the head, waving, pointing with one finger, etc.- would also be prohibited even when clearly done with no intention of devotional worship (*ibadah*). This type of logic is not a legitimate basis for establishing ruling in Shari'ah.

This logic makes no distinction between non-devotional customary (*al-'adah* or *'urf*) gestures of respect, recognition and association to a symbol - such as raising or saluting a flag; facing and circumambulating (*tawaf*) round the *Ka'bah*; touching, pointing or kissing the Black Stone; sitting or standing in front of a teacher or *imam*; having symbols on mosques and flags such as the crescent moon and star (of the Ottoman Caliphate); etc. - and devotional worship (*ibadah*) related gestures towards an image or idol, which is clearly prohibited (*haram*). An example of symbolism in devotional worship which represents disassociation and rejection is the "stoning of the devil" during the Hajj pilgrimage. This is in no way a basis for drawing an analogy with other different reasons for throwing stones at anyone or anything.

The validity of using analogical reasoning (*qiyas*) in Islamic law is dependent of the correctness in identifying the clear effective cause/reason (*'illah*) or wisdom (*hikmah*) behind the original action, and its similarity with the new case. In the case of raising the hands in *salah,* the reason for doing it is devotional worship (*ibadah*) while in the case of saluting a flag, it is not so. If saluting or raising a flag was done as an act of devotion and worship, then it would be regarded as prohibited (*haram*). Most acts of *ibadah* do not have clear and specific textually identified reasons (*'illah*). Scholars of Islamic law therefore generally do not approve of *qiyas* being applied to issues related to creed (*aqidah*) and prescribed devotional acts or rituals (*ibadah*).[127]

---

[127] Mohammad Hashim Kamali, Principle of Islamic Jurisprudence, p.191; Abdul WahabKhallaf, *Masadir al-Tashri' al-Islamiy fi ma la*

Additionally, physical movements that look exactly like acts of worship (*ibadah*) do not automatically become acts of *ibadah* unless they are preceded by a deliberate intention for the act to be an *ibadah* and done for that purpose. Consequently, washing of the limbs, face and head without the prerequisite intention for it as an act of *ibadah* does not constitute an ablution (*wudu*) for prayer (*salah*); abstinence from food and drink from dawn to sunset does not constitute fasting (*siyam*) without the prerequisite intention. The same applies to visiting specific sites at Makkah and pilgrimage (Hajj or Umrah), performing exercises or movements that are identical to those in prayer (*salah*); etc. The same also therefore applies to raising hands as in *salah* during *takbiratul ihram*. Raising one hand to salute a person or flag does not constitute an act of *ibadah* without the intention for it to be so. So while a posture like prostration (*sujud*) when done towards any other than Allah is prohibited by clear text irrespective of the intent, the salutation

---

Nass fihi, Kuwait, Dar al-Qalam, 1414 AH, 6th ed., p.26 and 30; Ibn Kathir, *Tafsir Ibn Kathir,* Dar Tayba, Madinah, 1420 AH, vol.7, p.465; Al-Hasan bin Ali al-Barbahari, *Sharh al-Sunnah,* Makrabah al-Sunnah, Egypt, 1416 AH, p.28, 47 & 49.

of a flag is not prohibited by any text nor is the act done with the intention of being an act of worship (*ibadah*). Intention for devotion or worship is therefore required to make a posture or gesture an act of *ibadah* or an act of *shirk* if it is directed to any other than Allah. The mere similarity of a posture or gesture with an act of *ibadah* is not sufficient to constitute an act of *shirk*.

There is therefore no basis in the Qur'an, Sunnah, practice of the Companions (*sahabah*), consensus (*ijma'*) or analogical deduction (*qiyas*) to prohibit the salutation of a flag, or to say that it is prohibited because it is somehow similar to raising of the hands in *salah* during *takbiratul ihram*. This therefore implies that there is no basis for such reasoning to be a criterion for declaring polytheism (*shirk*) or disbelief (*kufr*) on a person who salutes a flag or someone, even if one still regarded it as prohibited (*haram*).

22. Conventional Education is Prejudiced against Islamic Education

Traditional Islamic teachers who are learned scholars in the Islamic Sciences are discriminated against and not recognized by the conventional educational system simply because they do not understand English, even though some of them are more learned (about Islam) than those teaching in the universities and secondary schools. The educational system is therefore unjust and prejudiced against Islam and Muslim scholars (*Huffaz, Alaramomi, Gwani, and Malaman zaure*) by not recognizing them. Should Muslims continue to attend and support such institutions?

It is true that many professionals and especially those whose qualifications come along with titles tend to be arrogant and prejudiced against those whom they regard as beneath them. This is true for doctors (whether medical or academic) and barristers; as it is for engineers, professors, Imams and sheikhs.

Knowledge unfortunately usually comes with the challenge of pride, arrogance and prejudice.

The basis for a prohibition (*haram*) of something should be established on clear evidence from the Qur'an and Sunnah, and not on the attitudes or characters of people. The arrogance of a doctor, mechanic, teacher, school or institution does not make study of their field (medicine, engineering, etc.) to be *haram*. There are many Muslim scholars who have been unjust, prejudiced and discriminatory against others. Scholars of Hadith sometimes look down upon Scholars of the *Tafsir* of the Qur'an. Scholars of *Fiqh* sometimes feel superior to scholars of Hadith. Scholars of *Usul al-Fiqh* sometimes look down upon scholars of *Fiqh*. The knowledge of an arrogant or hypocritical Muslim Sheikh, Imam or scholar of Hadith or Qur'an does not mean that his knowledge or field of study is also *haram*. The discrimination, prejudice or arrogance of a scholar tells on the character of the scholar and not on the validity or otherwise of his field of expertise or knowledge of the subject. There is the need to always distinguish a person's behaviour from his subject, knowledge or institution.

Colonial powers have definitely been very prejudiced against Islam and Muslims. They have done whatever they can to undermine many of the traditional Muslim political, economic, judicial and educational institutions, and they have shown varying degrees of disregard for traditional scholars and scholarship. Muslims however now have the opportunity to change this through proper channels and methods, and reform these institutions to meet the needs of the Muslim Ummah today.

Many academic institutions, especially universities, recognize and offer honorary degrees to individuals who have excelled in their respective fields, even if these individuals do not speak English or have any degrees. Many Muslim scholars of various specializations have been given honorary PhDs and academic awards by conventional universities and professional institutions in Nigeria and beyond for their scholarship and contributions to Islam and the society. It is therefore not the university system as an institution that is necessarily prejudiced against the traditional institutions or its scholars, but some individuals within those institutions. More of these honourary degrees however need to be awarded to recognize and encourage competent traditional scholars of various specializations.

Meanwhile, it may also be asked whether there is also discrimination and prejudice by the traditional Islamic institutions and their scholars against those competent professors and lecturers in the conventional educational system. How many traditional Islamic institutions give similar recognition - through titles such as "Sheikh", "*Alaramma*", "Imam", etc. - to those distinguished academic scholars who have excelled in Islamic scholarship or even scholars of other fields that fulfill religiously mandated social or collective obligations (*fard kifayah*) such as teachers, doctors, agriculturists, engineers, etc.? Some university lecturers have earned recognition as proven authorities in both the Islamic and conventional systems of education.

There is however the need for building better linkages, collaboration and mutual respect between both types of institutions. In addition, better systems of identifying, assessing and evaluating competencies of talent in various specializations and levels of scholarship are needed.

Instead of prohibiting Muslims from attending conventional institutions, which have immense benefit to society, it may be better to encourage and support both systems of education to work better together wherever possible.

23. Western or Conventional Education amounts to Christianization

The Prophet (p) said: "Every child is born innately submitting to Allah (as a Muslim), it is his parents that change him to either be a Jew or a Christian or a Pagan". This hadith is understood to imply that taking children to any Western or conventional educational system is equivalent to "Christianizing" such children. What is the correct interpretation of this hadith?

This hadith is simply emphasizing the pure innate nature (*fitrah*) in which Allah has created all people, and the importance of parents in particular to the religious identity of most people. The hadith however does not discuss people raised by other than parents (as in orphanages), nor does it say that some people do not eventually choose whether or not to change their faiths later due to other external influences. It does not elaborate on other external influences besides the family such as friends, education, teachers, charismatic leaders, literature, media and the larger society, etc. It is therefore not correct to conclude that this hadith implies that it is prohibited for a Muslim to allow his/her children to get any education from non-Muslims, or that it implies that the parents have no influence over their own children anymore.

The fact that the Prophet (p) allowed Pagan (*mushrikun*) prisoners of the Battle of Badr to teach literacy to Muslims children,[128] makes it clear that there is no automatic prohibition of non-Muslims educating Muslims children, especially where there is no real fear of negative influences. In the case where there are legitimate fears of negative influences by non-Muslim (or even Muslim) teachers or fellow students, the parents and concerned Muslims who have intimate knowledge of the context and those involved would best advise what actions to take next.

However, the argument against sending children to certain schools may apply in those missionary schools

---

[128] Saifu al-Rahman al-Mubarakpuri, *Al-Rahiq Al-Makhtum (Sealed Nectar)*, Dar-us-Salam Publications, Riyadh, 1996, p.105

where children are actively converted to Christianity, and where the parents are insufficiently prepared to protect their children from the negative influences of the missionaries or of the school environment. However, this does not apply to all missionary schools or other private schools, nor does it apply to many government owned schools today. This argument can therefore not be used to prohibit Muslims from going to schools and acquiring education where this threat either does not exist, or where there are ways to effectively resist or counter such threats.

Parents always have the great responsibility of carefully assessing and monitoring the risk to their children and deciding what is best for them based on their assessment of risks and benefits. Allah instructs parents to *"Save yourselves and your families from the Fire!"* (Qur'an 66:6) Many Muslim children however, with the support of their parents and communities, have (with Allah's support) attended missionary schools that even actively but unsuccessfully tried to convert them to Christianity. Many of these children not only grew into proud Muslims, but were even able to convince some of their Christian colleagues to embrace Islam!

In the absence of better alternatives, Muslims are encouraged to establish their own schools for better socialization of their children, especially where that may be a better alternative in the estimation of the parents. Sometimes however, Muslim parents can have a greater influence on the school management if they played more active roles in the (Parents Teachers Association – PTA) of schools attended by their children.

Some Islamic organizations can play an active role in better influencing the educational system and school environment and making them conducive for the upbringing of Muslim children. These organizations include the Nigeria Association of Teachers of Arabic and Islamic Studies (NATAIS) and the MSSN among others.

24. Christian Dominated Schools as Christianizing Muslims

Western education is an avenue to convert Muslims to Christianity. In some government and Christian missionary controlled schools, there is pressure on Muslim children to convert to Christianity, and some Muslims children have left Islam. Is it permissible for Muslims to attend such schools when there is the risk of apostasy?

This question has been adequately addressed earlier while responding to Question No.23: "Western or Conventional Education amounts to Christianization"- above while discussing whether the Western or conventional educational system is equivalent to "Christianizing" Muslim children.

25. The Christian Origin and Identity of Academic Titles

Many titles in academic institutions have their origins in the titles of Christian clergy – such as Minister, Ministry, Chancellor, Dean, Doctor, etc. A Muslim should not use such names that identify him or her with another religion. Some say that to do so is prohibited and an act of disbelief (*kufr*). Is it permissible for a Muslim to use or be referred to with such religious titles? Is it permissible for a Muslim to work in institutions where such titles are used and awarded?

Not all primary, secondary or tertiary educational institutions use these titles. This argument, even if accepted cannot therefore be a justification for prohibiting Muslims from attending all modern educational institutions.

A basic rule and legal maxim in Shari'ah is that "Matters will be judged by their purposes" *(Al-umuru bi-maqasidiha).*[129] Therefore, those titles that fulfill religious purposes will be judged as religious while those that do not fulfill religious purposes will not be regarded as religious. All the academic titles used in educational institutions are not understood by anyone to carry or fulfill any religious function. Even subjects that have nothing to do with religions and those that may even be against Christianity carry such titles. The meaning and concept of Allah and Angels during the *Jahiliyyah* period was wrong. Islam retained the same words, but changed the meaning and concept to one that is correct. The present meaning is what the words "Allah" and *"mala'ikah"* (Angel) carry, and not their original or earlier meanings.

Another well-established legal maxim states that "With change in circumstances, comes change in

---

[129] Abdurahman bin Nasir al-Sa'di, *Risalah latifah fi Usul al-Fiqh al-Muhimma,* al-Maktabah al-Shamila, 3.13; Mohammad Hashim Kamali, *Qawa'id Al-Fiqh: The Legal Maxims of Islamic Law*, The Association Of Muslim Lawyers, U.K., 1998; Mohammad Hashim Kamali, *Principles of Islamic Jurisprudence*, The Islamic Text Society, Cambridge, 2003, p. 369-382; Mohammad Akram Laldin, *Introduction to Shari'ah and Islamic Jurisprudence*, 2nd ed. CERT, Kuala Lumpur, 2008, p.150-153. Umar Faruq Abd-Allah, *Living Islam with Purpose*, Nawawi Foundation, 2007, p.22-36

fatwah."[130] With the change in the nature of subjects and the fact that in present circumstances the titles have no religious connotation, the Islamic ruling on the use of these titles will also change.

Shari'ah is more concerned about the substance and reality of things and their implications than their form and names. Consequently, irrespective of the name of a thing, food, drink, title, person, transactions (*mu'amalat*), custom ('*urf*), fashion, etc., if the reality of that thing, its substantive nature and the implication of it is bad and harmful, Islamic law will prohibit it, even if it has a good name. This is called *Sadd al-dhari'ah*, which is about prohibiting things that are permissible in themselves, but which clearly lead to harm or haram. Similarly, even if something has a bad name, but its reality and substance is good, Shari'ah will permit it.

For instance, some fishes are called "Dogfish" or Catfish", "water pig", "water elephant" etc. We also have "non-alcoholic wine", etc. However, the real

---

[130] Ibn Qayyim al-Jawziyyah, *I'lam al-Muwaqqi'in*, Maktabat Kulliyah al-Azhariyyah, Cairo, 1968, vol. 3, p.47

nature and reality of these is that they are permissible (*halal*) irrespective of their names. Similarly, when a person is a "Minister of Petroleum", or "Dean of Administration", or "Doctor of Veterinary Medicine", "Chancellor of Usman Dan Fodio University", "Professor of Physics", etc., the fact is that no one regards the reality of these words as having anything to do with a religious purpose or role. They are therefore not prohibited.

In every field, industry, profession, academic, Islamic, etc. where people have different specializations and varying degrees of qualifications and competences, there is a need for an agreed upon system of positions and titles so as to help identify various specialists and experts. Where these titles are absent, it easily leads to deception and incompetent people pretending they know what they are doing, and those needing assistance being confused, distrustful and misguided.

Even if the argument is accepted as valid, the highest level of education and qualifications are required to bring sustainable changes to such titles in various institutions.

26. On Titles for Christian Clergy used for Muslim Scholars

The title "Doctor" used to describe an Islamic scholar is a Western terminology of Christian origin that is unknown in the Islamic sciences. What is traditionally known among Muslim scholars is Sheikh, Imam, *Hafiz, Muqri', Muhaddith, Mufassir, Faqih, Usuli, Mu'arrikh,* etc. Some Muslims are of the opinion that using the title "Doctor" while abandoning Muslim academic titles is an act of imitating non-Muslims (*tashbih*) and preferring their ways to those of the Islamic tradition. This is regarded by them as prohibited (haram). Is it permissible to a Muslim scholar to use the title "Doctor"?

This issue is similar to that treated earlier, Question No.25: The Christian Origin and Identity of Academic Titles.

The different titles used for various specializations of Islamic scholars –"Sheikh", "Imam", *"Hafiz", "Muqri'"*,

"Muhaddith", "Mufassir", "Faqih", "Usuli", "Mu'arrikh", "Sheikh ul-Islam", etc. – have not been prescribed by the Qur'an or Sunnah, and most of these were not used to describe even the most knowledgeable companions of the Prophet (p). It is therefore up to the community of scholars of each society and generation to choose the titles it wants for its various specializations and levels of qualifications. In order to improve cooperation within and between various communities, it is also important for scholars to agree on certain educational standards and titles.

The Western educational system borrowed terms and titles that were originally used in the church or Catholic educational system[131] and changed the use of these titles for experts in other subjects that had nothing to do with Christianity or religion. These terms therefore lost their purely religious significance and implication within the conventional educational systems and are therefore no longer religious or Christian but a part of non-religious culture (*'urf* and *'adah*).

---

[131] Bakr bin Abdullah Abu Zaid, *Al-Majmu'ah al-Ilmiyyah*, Tagrib al-Alqab al-Ilmiyya, Dar al-Asima, Riyadh, 1416 p.319

A "Doctor" (abbreviated "Dr.") is a title given to someone who has a PhD ("Doctor of Philosophy") or one who is competent in the field of human or veterinary (animal) medicine. It is also used as honourary title for anyone who has excelled in a particular field in the view of academic experts of that field. Because these titles are no more religious titles they are now similar to other titles such as "Architect", "Engineer", "Justice", "Chairman", "Major", "Minister", "Commissioner", "Emir", "Chief", etc. "Doctor" is used for various fields as a standard of high competence and is used by atheists and non-Christians. Using the title is therefore no longer an imitation (*tashbih*) of any religious title.

A basic rule and legal maxim in Shari'ah is that "Matters will be judged by their purposes" *(Al-umuru bi-maqasidiha).*[132] Therefore, those academic (or non-

---

[132] Abdurahman bin Nasir al-Sady, *Risalahun latifa fi Usul al-Fiqh al-Muhimma,* al-Maktabah al-Shamila, 3.13; Mohammad Hashim Kamali, *Qawa'id Al-Fiqh: The Legal Maxims of Islamic Law*, The Association Of Muslim Lawyers, U.K., 1998; Mohammad Hashim Kamali, *Principles of Islamic Jurisprudence*, The Islamic Text Society, Cambridge, 2003, p. 369-382; Mohammad Akram Laldin, *Introduction to Shari'ah and Islamic Jurisprudence*, 2nd ed. CERT,

academic) titles that fulfill religious purposes will be judged as religious while those that do not fulfill religious purposes will therefore not be regarded as religious.

Another well-established legal maxim states that "It cannot be denied that with change in circumstances, comes change in *fatwah*."[133] With the change in the nature of subjects and the fact that in present circumstances the titles have no religious connotation, the Islamic ruling on the use of these titles will also change from a prohibition to permissibility (*halal*).

Most Islamic scholars use both modern academic titles and traditional titles – such as Sheikh Dr. Yusuf al-Qaradawi. Even Sheikh Dr. Bakr Abu Zaid who is often quoted as being critical of the conventional educational system himself, has a Doctorate degree (PhD) from the Institute of Advanced Legal Studies (*Ma'had al-Ali lil Qada'a*) and he is addressed by the title "Doctor", and he did not allow the historical

---

Kuala Lumpur, 2008, p.150-153. Umar Faruq Abd-Allah, *Living Islam with Purpose*, Nawawi Foundation, 2007, p.22-36
[133] Ibn Qayyim al-Jawziyyah, *I'lam al-Muwaqqi'in*, Maktabat Kulliyah al-Azhariyyah, Cairo, 1968, vol. 3. p.47

origin of the title to prevent him from studying to PhD level.

It is therefore not prohibited by any text of the Qur'an, Sunnah, consensus (*'ijma'*) or analogy (*qiyas*) for a Muslim scholar to use academic titles that no longer have any un-Islamic religious implication. The absence of any prohibition is itself proof of permissibility (*halal*). In addition, Muslims may use traditional Islamic titles in addition to these if they so wish, or even come up with new titles if necessary.

The use of these titles is therefore not a basis for prohibiting Muslims for attending such academic institutions or working there and being referred to by these and other titles.

27. On Wearing Academic Gowns of Christian Clergy and Origin

Some Christian clergies originally used university convocation and academic gowns. It is prohibited from Muslims to use clothing that associates them with other religions as wearing such clothing is understood to be a form of imitation and association with their disbelief (*kufr*). Is it permissible for Muslim students or professionals to wear such clothing? Are those who wear such clothing committing *kufr* by imitating the disbelievers (*kuffar*)?

The Prophet (p) is reported to have said, *"He is not one of us who imitates a people other than us. Do not imitate the Jews and Christians."*[134] According to another version, *"Whoever imitates a people is one of them."*[135] It is along these lines that the distinguished scholar, Ibn Taimiyyah states:

> "People's sayings and actions are of two kinds: acts of worship by which their religion is established, and customary

---

[134] Al-*Tirmidhi*, No.1207
[135] *Musnad Ahmad*

practices which are required for day-to-day living. From the principles of the Shari'ah, we know that acts of worship are those acts which have been prescribed by Allah or approved by Him; nothing is to be affirmed here except through the Shari'ah. However, as far as the worldly activities of people are concerned, they are necessary for everyday life. Here the principle is freedom of action; nothing may be restricted in this regard except what Allah has restricted… to do otherwise is to be included in the meaning of His saying: *'Say: Do you see what Allah has sent down to you for sustenance? Yet you have made some part of it halal and some part haram?'* (Q.10:59)… Since this is the stance of the Shari'ah, people are free to buy, sell, and lease as they wish, just as they are free to eat and to drink what they like as long as it is not *haram* [prohibited]. Although some of these things may be disapproved, they are free in this regard, since the

> Shari'ah does not go to the extent of prohibiting them, and thus the original principle [of permissibility] remains."[136]

The answer to the question on wearing "Academic gowns" that were originally used by Christian clergy is similar to the answers given to Issues No.25: The Christian Origin and Identity of Academic Titles, and No.26: On Titles for Christian Clergy used for Muslims Scholars.

The academic gowns that are used within the conventional educational system and modern academic environment have lost their original and historically pure religious significance and implication. They are therefore no longer of religious or Christian significance, but now a part of non-religious academic culture (*'urf* and *'adah*) as they are used for and by every profession – Engineering, Medicine, Agriculture, History, Economics, Education, Pharmacy, Urban Planning, Geography, Architecture, etc. No one

---

[136] Ibn Taymiyyah, *Al-Qawa'id al-Nuraniyyah al-Fiqhiyyah*, pp.112-113, cited by Yusuf al-Qaradawi, *Lawful and the Prohibited in Islam* (London: Al-Birr Foundation, 2003), pp.5-6.

wearing such gowns or attire on an academic campus is assumed to be a member of the Christian clergy anymore because the purpose of the costume has changed. It is therefore not called a "Christian" or "Religious gown" but an "Academic", "Graduation" or "Matriculation gown", etc.

According to Sheikh Umar Faruq Abd-Allah, "the hadith –*"Whoever imitates (tashabbaha) a people is one of them."* - uses the verb "*tashabbaha*" (to imitate) instead of a related verb from the same root but with a different vowel pattern, "*tashābaha*" (to resemble). The former verb, "to imitate," stresses psychological motivation, especially the need to imitate a group other than one's own in order to be acceptable in their eyes. It reflects lack of self-esteem, feelings of inferiority, and a confused sense of identity.

As scholars have observed, it is notable that the Hadith does not use the latter form of the verb, "to resemble," because it would have fundamentally changed the meaning. The verb "to resemble" would have indicated that the mere act of being similar to others is disallowed, which is the mistaken interpretation that some Muslims give to the Hadith. By avoiding the latter verb, the Hadith shows that there is no harm in merely looking like others, as long as the act is not associated with the negative inward qualities indicated by the verb "to imitate." If a Muslim is motivated to wear the clothing of another people and imitate their customs out of a sense of inferiority, it is reprehensible. It is a different matter altogether when one wears the same clothing with self-esteem and the intention of being a functional member of society.[137]

The Prophet (p) wore some shoes that were similar or identical to what some Christian monks would wear.[138] As he was not trying to imitate (*tashbih*) them, the fact that they were similar also did not imply a prohibition. The fact that some Christian denominations and sects still wear such gowns now (similar to "academic gowns" in their own context),

---

[137] Umar Faruq Abd-Allah, *Living Islam with Purpose*, Nawawi Foundation, 2007, p.24

[138] Shaikh Abdullah bin Bayyah, *Sacred Law in Secular Lands* (Vol.1 and 2, 18 audio CDs), trans. from Arabic by Hamza Yusuf (California, USA: Alhambra Productions, 2000).

only shows a resemblance or similarity (*mushabahah*) with and not an imitation (*tashbih*) of Christian dressing.[139]

Similarly, the Prophet (p) said, *"The Jews and Christians do not pray in their khufoof (leather socks) or shoes, so be different from them"*, also, *"Distinguish yourselves from the Jews; they pray with their shoes off, so you should pray with your shoes on"*.[140] Some Jews and Christian groups still pray with their shoes off, while others go to church and pray with their shoes on. However, the fact that most Muslims and scholars pray(ed) with their shoes off in a similar way as these Jews or Christians do (or did) only shows resemblance (*mushabaha*) and not an imitation (*tashbih* or *tashabbaha*) since those Muslims who pray with their shoes off do so only so as not to dirty their prayer mats (*sajadah*) and sit down more

---

[139] For a discussion of the differences between similarity or resemblance (*mushaabaha/ tashaabaha*) and imitation (*tashbih/ tashabbaha*), see Umar Faruq Abd-Allah, *Living Islam with Purpose*, Nawawi Foundation, 2007, p.24; Shaikh Abdullah bin Bayyah, *Sacred Law in Secular Lands* (Vol.1 and 2, 18 audio CDs), trans. from Arabic by Hamza Yusuf (California, USA: Alhambra Productions, 2000).

[140] *Sunan Abu Dawud*, 652; *Sunan al-Baihaqi al-Kubra*, 4056

comfortably. Also, because some Christians now pray in church with their shoes on does not prove that those Muslims who do the same have decided to imitate these Christians. It only shows similarity and resemblance (*mushabaha*) which is permissible, and not imitation (*tashbih*) in order to look like or identify with them in a religious practice or costume which would be prohibited.

A basic rule and legal maxim in Shari'ah is that "Matters will be judged by their purposes" *(Al-umuru bi-maqasidiha).*[141] Therefore, those academic (or non-academic) gowns, hats, clothing, and symbols that fulfill religious purposes will be judged as religious. Those that do not fulfill religious purposes and are not used with the intent of religious identification will therefore not be regarded as religious.

---

[141] Abdurahman bin Nasir al-Sa'dy, *Risalahun latifa fi Usul al-Fiqh al-Muhimma*, al-Maktabah al-Shamila, 3.13; Mohammad Hashim Kamali, *Qawa'id Al-Fiqh: The Legal Maxims of Islamic Law*, The Association Of Muslim Lawyers, U.K., 1998; Mohammad Hashim Kamali, *Principles of Islamic Jurisprudence*, The Islamic Text Society, Cambridge, 2003, p. 369-382; Mohammad Akram Laldin, *Introduction to Shari'ah and Islamic Jurisprudence*, 2nd ed. CERT, Kuala Lumpur, 2008, p.150-153. Umar Faruq Abd-Allah, *Living Islam with Purpose*, Nawawi Foundation, 2007, p.22-36.

Another well-established legal maxim states that "It cannot be denied that with change in circumstances, comes change in *fatwah*."[142] With the change in the nature of the purpose and the fact that in present circumstances the gowns do not have an exclusively religious connotation, the Islamic ruling on the use of these gowns will also change from an earlier prohibition to permission (*halal*).

Some academic institutions use designs that are more similar to the traditional Arab gown (*al-kebbah*) used by some Muslims scholars, Arab leaders and elders.

The fact however still remains that distinguished scholars have and will continue to differ on this issue. Some regard wearing such academic gowns of historically Christian origin as still prohibited (*haram*), others regard them as discouraged (*makruh*), while others regard them as merely permissible (*mubah*). According to Sufyan At-Thawri,[143] *"If you see a man*

---

[142] Ibn Qayyim al-Jawziyyah, *I'lam al-Muwaqqi'in*, Maktabat Kulliyah al-Azhariyyah, Cairo, 1968, vol. 3. p.47

[143] He was also called the Amir al Mu'minin fi al-Hadith ("Leader of the Believer in Hadith") and was among the greatest scholars

doing something over which there is difference of opinion among scholars, and which you believe to be forbidden, you should not forbid him from doing it".[144]

Such issues upon which scholars continue to differ (*khilaf*) - and there are many others – should not be allowed to disunite the Ummah. They cannot and should not be a basis for abandoning the pursuit of an education or a school; nor is it a valid basis for attributing the sin of *shirk* or of declaring *kufr*.

It is narrated from Ibn Umar that the Prophet (p) said: "When a man calls his brother an unbeliever (*kafir*), it returns (at least) to one of them".[145] In other words, if you call a person a *kafir*, when he is not, then Allah will regard you as a *kafir*!

---

of the successors (*tabi'un*) of the companions of the Prophet (pbuh).
[144] Quoted in Abdal Hakim Murad, *Understanding the Four Madhahib* Cambridge: Muslim Academic Trust, 1999, p.13
[145] Ahmad, 4687; Al-Bukhari, 6103, Muwatta' Malik, 3606; Muslim, 224

"MINOR CONCERNS"

This section focuses on questions related to conventional education that are important to some, but not as regularly raised as those treated in the earlier section of this material.

28. The Un-Islamic Uniform Requirements for Muslim Boys at Maturity

A Muslim boy who has reached the age of maturity is required to have clothing that at least covers area from his navel to the knees. In many primary and junior secondary schools, male students are required to wear shorts that do not cover the knees. Is it permissible for Muslims students to attend such schools?

Refer to Question No.16 for more detail as the issue is similar.

Most boys reach puberty after finishing primary school. It is not prohibited for boys there to wear shorts or for girls there to not wear the hijab. Meanwhile some public and private primary schools still allow trousers for boys and hijabs for girls.

There is no generalization of this argument, as it does not apply to all schools. Many junior secondary schools accommodate trousers for boys.

Considering the greater needs of the Muslim *Ummah* and society as a whole, a school's prohibition of wearing trousers for boys does not justify good Muslim boys abandoning conventional education or all schooling altogether (*fard kifayah* and *fard ayn*). Choose the "lesser evil" when forced to choose between two evils.

There is a need to change school rules on dress code to accommodate religious freedom for all – an important role of the legal system, Human Rights lawyers, PTA, school staff, Government, community leaders, MSSN, NATAIS, Muslim Lawyers Association of Nigeria (MULAN), etc.

It should also be noted that some of the classical scholars of Islam, including Ahmad bin Hanbal, Imam Malik (in one narration), Ibn Jarir al-Tabari and some of the Zahiri scholars, have differed from the majority regarding whether the covering of the thighs of men is obligatory (*wajib*), or as these scholars maintain, only recommended (*mustahab*).[146] The existence of

---

[146] Muhammad bin Ali al-Shawkani, *al-Sail al-Jarrar*, Dar al-Kutub al-'Ilmiyya, Beirut, 1405AH, vol.1, p.160; Wahbah al-Zuhayli, *al-*

different opinions among scholars should make this issue not among the major priority issues of concern to the Ummah. And Allah knows best!

Fiqh al-Islami wa Adilatuhu, Dar al-Fikr, Damascus, vol.1, p.654-657; Abu Muhammad Ali bin Hazm, *al-Muhalla bi al-Athar*, al-Maktabah al-Shamilla 3.13, vol.3, p.210, Issue no.349; Ministry of Awqaf and Religious Affairs, *al-Mawsuat al-Fiqhiyyah al-Kuwaitiyyah*, Dar al-Salasil, Kuwait, 1404AH, vol.32, p.56

29. On the Educational System as the "Factory" of a Corrupt Nigeria

The society's corrupt leadership and elite – both Muslims and non-Muslims - are products of conventional schools. The conventional educational system has had the greatest educating influence on their upbringing. The moral and ethical corruption of the leadership has to be a product of the negative influence of the conventional educational system. Is it permissible to send Muslim children through such an educational system?

The Qur'an and Sunnah teach us that when we argue or speak, we should be fair and just – *"and if you speak, be just"* (Qur'an 6:152).

- *"O you who have attained to faith! Be ever steadfast in your devotion to God, bearing witness to the truth in all equity; and never let hatred of anyone lead you into the sin of deviating from justice. Be just; this is closest to being God-conscious. And remain conscious of*

> *God; verily, God is aware of all that you do."* (Qur'an 5:8)

- *"O you who have attained to faith! Be ever steadfast in upholding justice, bearing witness to the truth for the sake of God, even though it be against your own selves, or your parents and kinsfolk. Whether the person concerned be rich or poor, God's claim takes precedence over (the claims of) either of them. Do not, then, follow your own desires, lest you swerve from justice; for if you distort (the truth), behold, God is indeed aware of all that you do!"* (Qur'an 4:135)

It is true that some of our most corrupt Muslim and non-Muslim leaders are graduates from the conventional educational system, but so also are some of our best scholars and leaders (including Bakr Abu Zaid, Muqbil Al-Wadiy, Rabi al-Madkhali, Salih al al-Shaikh, Shaikh Abdullah bin Bayyah, amongst others) .Should we also attribute their goodness and moral quality to the same educational system, or to their parents, family and up-bringing; or the influence of good teachers and role models; or the good friends and colleagues they were lucky to have around them; or the good jobs they have; or their own self-restraint, moral resolve and commitment to decency; or to fear of the law, public embarrassment and loss of a good reputation; or to their God-consciousness, or is it all of the above? Or is it different for each individual and situation, and each individual is responsible for his or her moral behaviour?

Would it be fair to conclude that the fact that some *Islamiyyah* teachers (or "*mallams*") and scholars are also corrupt and morally bankrupt, means that their traditional Islamic educational system must be the cause as it is the "factory" that influenced their morals? Would it be fair to judge their educational system by those of them who abuse the ethics and ideals of that system – such as fortunetellers ("boka", "babalawo", etc.) and all other forms of fraudulent so-called "religious" people? This would not be fair either! Should that be a basis for prohibiting people from attending the traditional *Islamiyyah* or Arabic schools?

Is it also fair to single out the educational system as an important cause or as the "factory" responsible for our poor morals and ethical standards when the same educational system is used in many other Muslim and non-Muslim countries that do not have the level of corruption of Nigeria - such as Malaysia, Turkey, Iran, Qatar, Britain, Singapore, New Zealand, Australia, etc.?

There are many factors that influence or tempt individuals towards corruption and immoral behavior – economic, social, political, legal, psychological, etc. Some of these are related to their upbringing, while others are related to their environment. Most importantly however, while there are many influencing factors, Islam also recognizes the individual responsibility of every sane and mature adult. So, while various factors can and do influence us, we are ultimately still the determiners of our choices and behaviour. It was the same pre-Islamic (*Jahiliyyah*) society that the early Muslims and their Pagan contemporaries of Makkah grew up in, but each made and followed their own choices.

- "Indeed, We guided him to the way, be he grateful or be he ungrateful." (Qur'an 76:3)

- "And Satan will say when the matter has been concluded, "Indeed, Allah had promised you the promise of truth. And I promised you, but I betrayed you. But I had no authority over you except that I invited you, and you responded to me. So do not blame me; but blame yourselves. I cannot be called to your aid, nor can you be called to my aid. Indeed, I deny your association of me (with Allah) before. Indeed, for the wrongdoers is a painful punishment." (Qur'an 14:22)

This verse makes it explicitly clear that even Satan – the greatest tempter of humanity – has no power over us. We decide what to do with our choices and we cannot even blame him for our misguidance. We are to take full responsibility for our decisions.

Consequently, we cannot blame any of God's prophets for the misguidance of their family members or communities.

It is important to continue to do *da'wah*, by giving advice and finding better policies and ways of guiding parents, leaders, teachers and other role models to positively influence individuals towards enjoining what is right and forbidding wrong.

- *"O ye who believe! Save yourselves and your families from the Fire…"* (Qur'an 66:6)

- *"Every one of you is a shepherd (or leader) and each is responsible for his flock…"* (Bukhari and Muslim)

There is always the need for educational reform and improvement – along with the reforms of every other sector of society. There is also a need for better curricular and teaching methods that are geared to developing better character and morally upright and responsible people, and not just focus on pure academic progress. The need for preparing the next generation of leaders calls for a more holistic education.

However, the imperfections of the present system do not necessitate abandoning it, rather improving it to the best of our abilities. The benefit of even a poor education is still better than no education at all.

30. On Registration with Government as a Sign of Allegiance with *Kufr*

Some Muslims regard the registration of teachers, professionals, schools and organizations with the government as a sign of allegiance to *kufr*, and thus regard it as prohibited. Is it permissible for Muslims to register anything with the government?

It is on record that during the "Makkan Period" and within the legal system of the "*Jahiliyya* society" of Makkah, the Prophet (p) joined a group known as the **Hilf al-Fudul**. This was a group of upright individuals in Makkah who would stand to protect the rights of any victim of oppression in Makkah. Even after Islam was well-established, the Prophet (p) recounted his involvement with the Hilf al-Fudul, and according to Talha bin Abdullah, he said that "if I was to be invited again to join such as group now in the time of Islam, I would respond and join them".[147] According to Ibn Hisham, "They (members of Hilf al-Fudul) promised and pledged that they would not find any oppressed person among their people or among anyone else who

---

[147] Sunan Al-Kubra, no.12114; *Al-Dala'il fi Gharib al-Hadith*, 243

entered Makkah except that they would support him. They would stand against whoever oppressed him until the rights of the oppressed were returned."[148] The Prophet (p) was reported by Ibn Abbas as having said, "Every pact (or treaty) from the Time of Ignorance (*Jahiliyyah*) is not increased by Islam except in strength and affirmation."[149] Such an allegiance, commitment and pledge to work for the common good (*maslahah*) in collaboration with non-Muslims is not viewed as giving allegiance to disbelief (*kufr*), since there is no compromising of Islamic values. It is in fact more effectively promoting the purposes (*maqasid*) of Shari'ah.

Scholars have concluded from this that Muslims, even where they do not control the government or laws of the land, are expected to enjoin right and forbid wrong (as instructed by the Qur'an 3:104) to the best of their abilities (Qur'an 64:16) within the existing societal restrictions. Allah says Muslims should

---

[148] Ibn Hisham, *Sirat an-Nabawiyyah*, 1/123; *Al-Dala'il fi Gharib al-Hadith*, 243
[149] *Musnad Ahmad*, 2904

"Cooperate in righteousness and piety, and do not cooperate in sin and aggression" (Qur'an 5:2).

Even if registration of an organization or school with the relevant government authorities was interpreted as a sign of an alliance with a non-Muslims government, it would be permissible since it brings mutual benefit (*maslahah*), it does not contradict the Shari'ah, and it is actually in line with the *Sunnah*. In addition, it is neither an alliance with the ideology of *Kufr* nor an allegiance to it.

Registration of schools and other organizations is usually for the purpose of good governance, quality control and standardization in the public interest (*maslahah*). It is to ensure easy oversight, monitoring and regulation of standards in various fields. This protects the society against unqualified professionals - doctors, pharmacists, engineers, architects, students, teachers, landowners, drivers, judges, electricians, technicians, security personnel, etc. It allows the leadership to easily know and contact legitimate and qualified individuals and groups. It makes the tracking of crimes and dubious accounts easy. It also facilitates information and data collection, statistics and demographics which the relevant levels of leadership can use for budgeting and planning resource allocation. This is in line with Islam's encouragement of orderliness (*nizam*), enabling or accruing benefit (*jalb al-masalih*) and prevention of harm (*dar'ul mafasid*). None of these contradict the teachings of the Qur'an and Sunnah. They actually facilitate the realization of the purposes and objectives (*maqasid*) of Shari'ah.

During times of crisis, there is usually a need to regulate preaching and public enlightenment to ensure that only those competent and qualified to handle such responsibilities do so. The registration of various institutions makes it easier for government or the relevant agencies to perform their jobs more efficiently and reduce social strife (*fitnah*).

The Prophet (p) and his companions went into hundreds of peace, trade and security treaties, alliances and pacts with various groups including Idol worshippers or Pagans (such as the *Mushrikun* or *Kuffar* of Makkah during the Treaty of Hudaibiyyah, and the pagan tribe of Banu Thaqif, etc.), Jews (such as the Jews of Madinah and Banu Nadir, etc.), Christians (such as the Christians of Najran and Banu Taghlib, etc.), and many others form Persia (Zoroastrians/*Majus*), Egypt (Coptic Christians), Roman/Byzantine (Eastern Orthodox Christians), etc. The allegiance to such treaties and alliances for peace and collaboration were with the *Mushrikun, Ahl al-Kitab* (and *Kuffar*) as a people. They were not in any way regarded as an acceptance and belief in the truthfulness of their ideology of polytheism (*shirk*) or of disbelief (*kufr*). Treaties and alliances with non-Muslims for the purpose of mutual benefit (*maslahah*) are therefore permissible for Muslims based on the practice (*sunnah*) of the Prophet (p) and his Rightly Guided companions.[150]

When Muslims live in any place that is governed by laws that are not guided by Islamic teachings, as did the companions in Abyssinia (Ethiopia) or in Makkah

---

[150] For more examples of treaties by the Prophet (pbuh) and his companions with various non-Muslim communities, see Shaikh-ul-Islam Dr. Muhammad Tahir-ul-Qadri, *Fatwa on Terrorism and Suicide Bombing*, Minhaj-ul-Quran International, London, 2010, p.141-156.

(after the treaty of Hudaibiyyah) during the time of the Prophet (p), they are to work within the existing legal system and peace treaty agreements (*sulh*) to bring about better changes. Even the King (Negus) of Ethiopia at the time, who had embraced Islam, was not in a position to implement any other laws other than the customary law of the land.

The Prophet (p) instructed Muslims and their leadership to always honour and stand by the agreements they make: "Muslims are bound by the conditions they accept" ("*Al Muslimun inda shurutihim!*"),[151] and all believers are characterized in the Qur'an as those "*who are faithful to their trusts and to their pledges*" (Qur'an 23:8). Again, Allah says, "*And fulfil (every) covenant. Verily, the covenant will be questioned about*" (Qur'an 17:34), and "*O you who believe! Fulfil (your) obligations*" (Qur'an 5:1).

The allegiance and commitment to an alliance of both Muslims and non-Muslims is therefore not regarded

---

[151] *Al-Tirmidhi*, 1352

as disbelief (*kufr*) since it is meant for mutual benefit (*maslahah*) and does not harm Muslims.

A society or nation that is not governed by Islamic law but by laws that represent a compromise for peace with non-Muslim citizens is usually referred to by scholars as an "Abode of Treaty" (*Dar al-Sulh*). It is permissible for Muslims to live in such lands and they are to respect the laws that the treaty or constitution agreed upon by the leadership of the communities involved – such as Abyssinia even after the *Hijrah* migration; Makkah during the Treaty of Hudaibiyyah; and the very many non-Muslim communities and areas where Muslims have established treaties (*sulh*) of peaceful relations and mutual cooperation, etc.

The registration of schools and various other organizations and institutions with the government for the purpose of bringing public benefit (*jalb al-masalih*) and removing harm and corruptions (*dar' al-mafasid*) is permissible and should be encouraged. To support the opposite (non-registration and deregistration), undermines transparency and good oversight. It also opens the doors to various forms of corruption and exploitation of innocent people.

31. Making Teachers Stand in Class as a Sign of Disrespect

In the traditional Islamic educational system, it is more respectful of teachers and their status that they sit down while teaching students who will be seated on the floor. In conventional education, the teacher is required to stand up and move around, while the students are relaxed in their chairs. This is a sign of disrespect towards the teacher and his knowledge. Is it permissible for Muslims to attend such classes and institutions?

The Sunnah of the Prophet (p) and that of his companions was for the Imam to stand up when giving a sermon (*khutbah*) such as during the Friday or *Eid* prayers and the congregation remain seated on the floor. In a number of hadiths, the Prophet (p) or Caliph would also stand up to speak or give advice, etc., in the mosque while the congregation was seated. Standing was not seen by the Prophet and his companions as a sign of humiliations, nor was sitting a sign of disrespect. Consequently, most public lecturers give their presentations while standing while the audience are seated.

As the speaker is often the only one speaking at a time and who needs to be more visible and seen by the audience, it makes sense that he or she is standing. This increases the attention and concentration given to the presentation. It also makes it easier for the audience to listen to many different teachers or speakers (or to long speeches) without quickly getting tired. Some students are in school for over 5 hours! Very often, a chair is also made available for a teacher or lecturer in case he or she needs to sit down too. It is also the choice of the teacher to stand or sit depending on his or her preference. If they have to use a white or blackboard and to move around the class to observe the students better, then it makes sense that he/she is standing. If the student has something to say, it makes sense too that they also stand up to speak. If all students or audiences were to remain standing when a teacher was speaking, it would be difficult for those at the back to see the teacher or the board. It would also make it more difficult for the teacher to observe each of them.

The seating and standing arrangements in a class are therefore not a sign of disrespect but of fulfilling functionality and achieving the objectives of education. Schools and teachers are free to come up with whatever arrangements they consider best for their various purposes.

The Qur'an and Sunnah have therefore not prescribed any specific posture for teachers and students when learning, and there is no evidence from the Shari'ah to suggest that Islam views it as disrespectful for people to be sitting while they are learning from a teacher. Such judgments are therefore based on cultural perception and preferences ('urf and 'adah) and should not be presented as Islamic teachings when they contradict the Sunnah, otherwise they are to be regarded as heretical innovations in the religion (bid'ah).

32. On Caliph Umar Discouraging Learning in Other than Arabic

It is narrated that Umar bin Khattab discouraged the learning of languages other than Arabic.[152] Most conventional schools do not teach in Arabic. Should attending these schools not be at least discouraged for Muslims?

The answer to this question is similar to No.3: On Giving less Attention to Religious Education in Schools.

Arabic is the language of the Qur'an and hadith and most of the classical writings by scholars. It is the language in which we perform our prayers (*salah*) and many supplications (*du'a*). It is therefore important for Muslims to learn at least some basic Arabic so they understand better what they are saying; especially in their prescribed prayers. One of the reasons given for the prohibition of coming to prayer while intoxicated is that they will not know what they are saying; *"O you who have believed, do not approach prayer while you*

---

[152]Ahmad bin Abdul Halim bin Taimiyyah, *Iqtida' al-Sirat al-Mustaqim*, Matba'at al-Sunnah al-Muhammadiyyah, Cairo, 1369AH, p.135

are intoxicated until you know what you are saying…" (Qur'an 4:43). It is therefore important for Muslims to know and understand what they are saying in prayers!

As Islam was expanding, the Caliph Umar was naturally concerned that a loss in the quality of Arabic language of the people and its adulteration with other languages would imply a loss in the quality of understanding of Islam. Umar's actions were in no way prohibiting people from learning other languages, nor did it imply that Arabs were in any way better than non-Arabs simply based on their language or race.

The Prophet (p) in fact sent Zaid bin Thabit to learn Hebrew[153], the language of the Jews, which he did along with learning Persian (*Farsi*). As the Prophet (p) was sent to all of humanity, Islam has spread as a global religion to humanity through other languages and translations of the Qur'an and other texts.

Scholarship and the learning of Arabic for the purpose of preserving the proper understanding of the Qur'an

---

[153] *Sunan al-Tirmidhi*, 2715

and Sunnah is a collective social obligation (*fard kifayah*) and not an individual obligation (*fard ayn*). Therefore, if there are some people who pursue such scholarship and proficiency in Arabic, it suffices to fulfill that obligation, and allows other people to focus on their other obligations and responsibilities. It is not compulsory for everyone to learn Arabic, and therefore it is not wrong to go to a school where Arabic is not taught. There are many other opportunities provided by various private and public organizations and institutions for mastering Arabic. Some of these are online and free, while others need to be paid for.

- o All languages are among the signs and wonders of Allah;*"Among His signs is the creation of the heavens and the earth and the diversity of your languages and your colors. Verily, in that are signs for people of knowledge."*(Qur'an 30:22)

- o *"O mankind, indeed We have created you from male and female and made you peoples and tribes that you may know one another..." (Qur'an 49:13)

- Abu Nadrah reported that the Prophet (p) said, *"O people, your Lord is one and your father Adam is one. There is no virtue of an Arab over a foreigneror a foreigner over an Arab, and neither white skin over black skin or black skin over white skin, except by righteousness. Have I not delivered the message?"*[154]

- The Prophet (p) also said, *"He is not one of us who calls to tribalism. He is not one of us who fights for the sake of tribalism. He is not one of us who dies following the way of tribalism."*[155]

While learning Arabic is useful and important for many reasons, other languages are also very important for greater exposure to the useful knowledge Allah has shared throughout humanity and human history - for commerce, cooperation,

---

[154] *Musnad Ahmad*, 22978.
[155] *Sunan Abu Dawud*, 5102.

diplomatic and other personal reasons, and for sharing the message of Islam with others (*da'wah*).

33. Some Mathematical Symbols are similar to the Cross or Crucifix

Multiplication and addition symbols in mathematics are similar in shape with the cross or a crucifix. Is learning and using such symbols permissible in Islam, or is it an act of disbelief ("*kufr*")?

The answer to this question is similar to No.27: On Wearing Academic Gown of Christian Clergy and Origin.

The existence of similarities between symbols is not proof of imitation (*tashbih*), it only shows commonality or resemblance (*mushabahah*) which is not prohibited.

In addition, the symbols for addition and multiplication do not represent religious symbols nor are they used for such purposes by anyone of any religious or non-religious affiliation. The fact that they look similar to a cross or crucifix does not make them represent Christianity. Even Christians do not recognize these mathematical symbols as representing their faith.

A basic rule and legal maxim in Shari'ah is that "Matters will be judged by their purposes" *(Al-umur bi-maqasidiha)*.[156] Therefore, those symbols that fulfill religious purposes will be judged as religious while those that do not fulfill religious purposes and are not used with the intent of religious identification will therefore not be regarded as religious.

That the letters "C" and "D" in English look like a crescent moon does not make them religious symbols. Nor does the fact that the number '3' in Arabic which looks like the Hindu Trident of the goddess Shiva make it haram to be used. Just because a student draws a 5 or 6-sided star which looks like the Star of David does not make it a religious/Jewish symbol nor does it imply that he or she is imitating Judaism! Likewise, just because the number "5" in Arabic looks like zero in English does not mean they are the same or related.

---

[156] Abdurahman bin Nasir al-Sady, *Risalahlatifah fi Usul al-Fiqh al-Muhimmah,* al-Maktabah al-Shamila, 3.13; Mohammad Hashim Kamali, *Qawa'id Al-Fiqh: The Legal Maxims of Islamic Law*, The Association Of Muslim Lawyers, U.K., 1998; Mohammad Hashim Kamali, *Principles of Islamic Jurisprudence*, The Islamic Text Society, Cambridge, 2003, p. 369-382; Mohammad Akram Laldin, *Introduction to Shari'ah and Islamic Jurisprudence*, 2nd ed. CERT, Kuala Lumpur, 2008, p.150-153. Umar Faruq Abd-Allah, *Living Islam with Purpose*, Nawawi Foundation, 2007, p.22-36

There is also a fatwah from the Permanent Fatwah Council of Saudi on the permissibility of using these mathematical symbols.[157]

The similarity of the multiplication and addition signs with a cross or crucifix is therefore not an acceptable excuse in Shari'ah for not using them or for discouraging the study of mathematics.

---

[157] *Fatwah al-Lajnah al-Dai'mah;al-Majmuatu al-Thaniyah*, Fatwa no.18441

34. On Professors of Islamic Studies who Cannot Recite the Qur'an Properly

Some lecturers and professors of Islamic studies in Nigeria cannot even properly recite the Qur'an in Arabic, and have memorized very little of it. Can a person who does not understand Arabic be regarded as a scholar, or have the authority to teach Islam? Is it permissible to learn Islam from Institutions with such lecturers?

This is a rare occurrence and cannot be used to judge all the lecturers or departments of Islamic Studies in conventional universities. And while it is a weakness that is found with some lecturers, positive changes are taking place and such a problem is getting less common than it was in the past.

Islamic Studies is a broad subject with various specializations requiring varying levels of competence in Arabic. Because many of the important literatures relevant to some specializations have been translated into English, French or German, it has become easy for those who know some of these languages to have access to a lot of information on subjects such as Islamic History, Islamic Philosophy, Contemporary Islamic Movements, Islamic Ethics, and some aspects of Islamic law, etc. Some lecturers have therefore been able to acquire PhDs and become professors without having to learn Arabic to a significant level. They therefore have also qualified to lecture in those specific aspects of Islamic studies but not others.

Other lecturers who handle subjects such as the Sciences of the Qur'an (*Ulum al-Qur'an*), the Sciences of Hadith (*Ulum al-Hadith*), Islamic jurisprudence and law (*Fiqh*), etc. are usually very proficient in classical Arabic.

Some students of Islamic studies are also proficient in Arabic and are free to write their projects and thesis in Arabic, in some Nigerian universities. Some students also take courses in Arabic language from the Arabic Studies departments of their universities.

Meanwhile, Abu Ishaq Al-Shatibi is reported to have said,

"When *ijtihad* relates to inferring from the Qur'an or Sunnah text, a knowledge of Arabic would be essential. But if the focus is not the purpose of the text but a conceptualization of the *masalih* and *mafasid* involved, a knowledge of Arabic may not be essential….Whosoever has come to understand what are the purposes of giving rulings in Shari'ah and is so advanced in this understanding, that he could be regarded as knowing what the objectives of Shari'ah are, (for him) it makes no difference at all if he acquired that knowledge through translations in some of the non-Arabic tongues. He and the one who acquired the understanding from Arabic readings are at par".[158]

A Muslim student should bear in mind that any specialist in one field is often a layperson in another field. An expert in a subject often knows a lot about a

---

[158] Abu Ishaq al-Shatibi, *Al-Muwafaqat fi Usul al-Shari'ah*, Cairo, Egypt, Al-Maktabah al-Tawfiqiyyah, 2003, vol.3, pp.162-163. Cited in Mohammad Omar Farooq, *Towards Our Reformation: From Legalism to Value Oriented Islamic Law and Jurisprudence*, IIIT, London, 2011, p.xiv

very narrow area of knowledge. It is therefore more reasonable not to expect a lecturer in one field to know a lot about many others. It is wise for the student and anyone for that matter to listen to what is taught and take the best of it, while excusing mistaken statements by lecturers in fields other than their fields of specialization. Allah praises those who listen critically and pick what is best from what they learn: *"those who listen to what is said, and go by the best in it."* (Qur'an 39:18)

The poor Qur'anic recitation and memorization of a few lecturers or professors of Islamic Studies should not prevent anyone from learning other useful knowledge from these lecturers, or from others in the department.

35. On the Hadith: "We are an Ummah that is illiterate...nor do we calculate"

The Prophet (p) is reported to have said: *"We are an Ummah that is illiterate; we don't write or calculate."* The Qur'an also describes the Prophet (p) as an "illiterate" (*nabiy al-ummiyy*). These texts show that we do not need to go to school to learn literacy or numeracy. Is it therefore not prohibited for Muslims to go to educational institutions that teach these skills?

If this understanding and implication of these texts is correct, then why did the Prophet (p) ask some of his respected companions and scribes to write down the Qur'an from his dictation?; Why did the Prophet (p) put as a condition for the freedom of the literate prisoners of the Battle of Badr, that they each teach 10 Muslim children literacy?; Why would the Qur'an include injunctions to write down business loans, wills or bequests, and other agreements? (Qur'an 2:282, 4:12); Why would the Qur'an require knowledge of fractions and percentages in the calculation of inheritance, *zakat,* and other taxes? (Qur'an 4:11-12,

4:176); Why did the Prophet (p) get letters written to leaders of other nations and communities? Why did the Prophet (p) agree to written treaties and alliances with various other communities? Why did all our great scholars from the earliest generation (*salaf*) to the later (*khalaf*) learn how to read and write the volumes they produced? Why did the scholars of hadith literature develop their literary skills and compile so many hadith if literacy was wrong? etc.

The interpretation of this hadith therefore must be wrong as it contradicts the reality of the understanding of the importance of literacy and numeracy in the life of the Prophet (p) and his companions and in Islamic history and scholarship.

The more complete wording and context of the hadith makes the meaning and implication clearer:

> It was narrated from Abdullah bin 'Umar that the Prophet (p) said: *"We are an unlettered nation, we do not write or calculate. The month is such-and-such or such-and-such –*

> *meaning sometimes it is twenty-nine and sometimes it is thirty."*[159]

The hadith was narrated in the context of a discussion on ways of determining the beginning of the new lunar month which is known to always have either 29 or 30 days. The statement was made to explain that the community should rely on sighting of the moon and not on calculations. It did not come to urge the *ummah* to remain ignorant of writing skills or of arithmetic and all other useful sciences. Literacy and numeracy are in fact a collective obligation (*fard kifayah*) which some members of any Muslim community must have!

Shaikh al-Islam Ibn Taymiyyah wrote a very useful comment on this hadith:

> "The phrase 'We are an unlettered nation' is not telling them to be like that. They were unlettered before Islam came, as Allah says (interpretation of the meaning):

---

[159] Bukhari, 1814; Muslim, 1080

> *"He it is Who sent among the unlettered ones a Messenger (Muhammad) from among themselves"* (Qur'an 62:2)
>
> *"And say to those who were given the Scripture (Jews and Christians) and to those who are illiterates (Arab pagans): Do you (also) submit yourselves (to Allah in Islam)?"* (Qur'an 3:20)
>
> Although this is how they were before the Prophet (p) was sent to them, they were not commanded to remain like that."[160]

In other words, the statement was descriptive and not prescriptive. The purpose of the Prophet (p) saying "We are an unlettered nation. We do not write nor do we calculate" was simply to describe the reality of the state of the majority of the Arab nation at his time. The statement was made to emphasize why he therefore rejected the more speculative astronomical calculations used for determination of the new lunar month, in favour of the easier, more apparent and

---

[160] *Majmu' al-Fatwahs*, 25/164-175

certain method of visual sighting of the new moon which most people were already used to.

From the context of the hadith and other relevant texts, and the understanding of Muslim scholars from the earliest period, it is clear that it is not prescribing that Muslims should be illiterate or innumerate.

These texts cannot therefore be used to discourage others from any form of education.

And Allah knows best!

Conclusion

From the foregoing, various arguments used by some to justify the non-adoption of conventional education have been considered and addressed. There are arguments that have to do with the curriculum content such as the teaching of unislamic subjects and the absence of religious teachings in some schools. Some arguments border on the moral decadence in many educational institutions and its corrupting influence on the society. Likewise, some oppositions are hinged on the perceived Christianizing effects of conventional education; as well as the unislamic nature of some school uniforms.

It is noteworthy that some of these arguments are significant, as some of the current educational policies and provisions do not sufficiently take into account the sensibilities of Muslims. While some Muslims can afford to overlook the inadequacies of the current system, many cannot. Hence, there is need for redress. However, just as we do not throw the baby away with the bath water, so also should we not reject conventional education totally because of the current shortfalls. Rather, all hands should be on deck to ensure that there are changes in policies and provisions that would be more accommodating of Muslim sensibilities. Such actions include:

- Muslim parents and the leadership should ensure that what is not learnt at school or in one school (or through one teacher) is learnt elsewhere – home, afternoon classes, mosque, weekends, holidays, etc. In some places, a student can go to the school in the morning and *Islamiyyah* in the afternoon; or attend Islamic camping programmes and other beneficial lectures. Parents especially have a critical role to play in ensuring that their children learn their religion - e.g. Qur'an, *Salah*, morals and ethics - from reliable sources.

- There should be more *da'wah* for Muslims to be cognizant of *haram* and avoid misusing their qualifications for immoral purposes.

- While various environments such as schools, markets, communities, and other organizations and institutions may have various levels of evil and corruption in them, good Muslims must not leave these places to be fully under the control of immoral people. They must effectively resist evil and struggle towards changing things for the better in the long term as did the Prophet (p) and his companions, and all the great scholars.

- While coeducational institutions are Islamically acceptable as already explained, parents may still enroll their children in single-sex schools meant for only boys or only girls, if that would be better and safer.

- There is however the need for more qualified Muslims in the field of Law and Human Rights who are competent enough to take legal action against bigots, extremists and others who would want to deny Muslims (or anyone else) of their legally protected religious freedoms (e.g. of wearing hijab).

- There is the need for more female security personnel and examination invigilators to inspect and verify the identity of *niqab*-wearing students. This naturally also implies the need for more educated Muslim female professionals in security services.

- There is the need for building better linkages, collaboration and mutual respect between Muslim academics and traditional Islamic scholars; along with better systems of assessing and evaluating competences, and the identification of talent and distinction in various specializations and levels of scholarship.

- While it is best that Muslim parents should send their children to Muslim owned schools, where children have to attend schools owned by non-Muslims, Muslim parents can have a greater influence on the school management if they played more active roles in the Parents Teachers Association (PTA) of schools attended by their children.

- There is need to change relevant school rules on dress code to accommodate religious freedom for all – an important role of the legal system, Human Rights lawyers, Parents and Teachers Associations (PTA), school staff, government, community leaders, Muslim Students Society of Nigeria (MSSN), National Association of Teachers of Arabic and Islamic Studies (NATAIS), *Jama'atu Nasril Islam* (JNI), Association of Model Islamic Schools (AMIS), *Nasrul-Lahi-l-Fatih* Society (NASFAT), Federation of Muslim Women Association in Nigeria (FOMWAN), Women in Da'awah (WID), Muslim Sisters Organizations (MSO), Muslim Public Affairs Centre (MPAC), Da'awah Coordination Council of Nigeria (DCCN), *Jama'atu Izalati Bid'ah wa Iqaamati Sunnah* (JIBWIS), National Council of Muslim Youth Organizations (NACOMYO), Muslim Lawyers Association of Nigeria (MULAN), and interfaith organizations, amongst others.

- There is always the need for educational reform and improvement – along with the reforms of every other sector of society. There is also the need for better curricular and teaching methods that are geared towards developing better character and morally upright and responsible people, and not just a focus on pure academic progress. The need for preparing the next generation of leaders calls for a more holistic education.

While we acknowledge that the arguments contained in this book are not exhaustive, we have tried to cover the most important and popular ones, to the best of our ability. We hope that by taking actionable steps, following the recommendations given above, and others that may be suggested, we would be able to have a more advanced Ummah that would be able to do more for humanity, by Allah's leave.

Alhamdulillahi Rabbil 'Alamin

Other Books By The Publisher

1. Authenticity of the Qur'an
2. Understanding Misconceptions About Islam
3. What is "Islamic Culture"?
4. Relations with Non-Muslims
5. Should Muslim Women Speak?
6. Muslim Women in the Public Space
7. The Hijab Q & A
8. Is Polygamy Fair to Women?
9. Jihad and the Spread of Islam
10. Sharing Islam through Dialogue
11. To Veil or Not to Veil?
12. Saying Salam to Non-Muslims

13. Protection of Churches, Synagogues and Mosques

14. Shari'ah Intelligence

www.ingramcontent.com/pod-product-compliance
Lightning Source LLC
Chambersburg PA
CBHW082005060426
42449CB00036B/3244